WAN Optimization with Riverbed

2018 Edition

Deploying Riverbed® SteelHead® Appliances to Accelerate Application Performance across the Wide Area Network

By Nolan Chen

Contents

Preface to 2018 Edition

As wide area networks continue to evolve, so does the need to update "WAN Optimization with Riverbed." While the core technology underlying Riverbed WAN Optimization has remained unchanged, Riverbed appliance models have continued to evolve to meet the new requirements of WANs connected to public and private clouds. The 2018 edition of "WAN Optimization with Riverbed" adds new content on SteelHead SaaS, SteelHead Cloud and SteelHead for SteelConnect while dropping coverage on the older xx50 and EX Series appliances.

Introduction

Just as the telegraph and then the telephone conquered communication distance in prior centuries, WAN optimization today has virtually eliminated distance between mobile workers, branch offices and cloud data centers located around the world. It enables companies to build out their IT infrastructure with better performance and for less cost.

This book is an introduction to WAN optimization and how Riverbed® solutions are used to deliver WAN optimization. It is intended for the CIO, Network Administrator and the IT professional who has been tasked with implementing WAN optimization for his or her organization. This book covers the most common scenarios in WAN optimization based on the author's ten plus years of experience with Riverbed. It aims to help the reader to ramp up quickly in understanding what's needed in order to implement a WAN optimization solution.

Chapter 1 of this book gives an introduction to WAN optimization. It reviews the challenges of delivering IT performance over the Wide Area Network and how delivering greater performance can bring tremendous benefits for organizations.

Chapter 2 of this book introduces the Riverbed Optimization System or RiOS®. RiOS is the software that powers Riverbed's market leading SteelHead appliances for WAN optimization. We discuss the techniques used by RiOS to deliver superior application performance across the WAN.

Chapter 3 introduces Riverbed's SteelHead appliance product family for WAN optimization. It includes coverage on SteelHead SaaS, SteelHead Cloud as well as SteelFusion Edge.

Chapter 4 describes the different options for deploying SteelHead appliances. We present the differences between an in-path, out of path and virtual in-path deployment. We also discuss the pros and cons of each option.

Chapter 5 of this book gives "hands on" instructions for installing and configuring SteelHead appliances. Here we give step by step instructions for implementing the most common tasks with SteelHead appliances as well as how to deploy SteelHead SaaS.

Chapter 6 gives tips on how troubleshoot common issues that occur when deploying SteelHead appliances.

Armed with the knowledge in this book, the reader should have a clear understanding of what WAN optimization can do for his or her organization and how this technology can be implemented using Riverbed SteelHead appliances.

Chapter 1: WAN Optimization

What is WAN optimization?

The following definition of WAN optimization can be found in Wikipedia:

"...a *collection of techniques for increasing data-transfer efficiencies across wide-area networks*"

Note that WAN optimization is "a collection of techniques." It is not just one method or technology. This collection of techniques is implemented across the different layers of the network stack and they are constantly evolving. We shall discuss these different techniques in more detail.

And what does WAN optimization do? It results in "increasing data-transfer efficiencies across wide-area networks." These increases in efficiencies result in dramatic benefits which can be described as the "ABCDs of WAN optimization."

ABCDs of WAN optimization

The benefits of WAN optimization can be summarized as the "ABCDs" of WAN optimization:

- Application Acceleration
- Bandwidth Savings
- Consolidation
- Disaster Recovery & Replication

Application Acceleration

IT applications have become an integral part of our everyday lives. How many of us can make it through a single work day without reading email, opening a document file or accessing a web application? With our dependence on IT applications comes the need for faster performance.

The following is a partial list of the types of applications which can benefit from WAN optimization:

- File Sharing
- Web Applications
- Email
- FTP
- Data Backup & Replication
- Remote & Virtual Desktop
- Software as a Service (SaaS)

WAN optimization makes the "WAN feel like a LAN." With WAN optimization, engineers located in different parts of the world can collaborate and work together on large project files as if they were in the same office. Large databases can now be backed up to secondary sites located thousands of miles away without having to first back them up to tape and then transported by truck. Mobile workers connecting their laptops into their corporate VPN can download email half a world away just as fast as if they were in the office.

In short, application acceleration virtually eliminates distance between workers. It saves precious time and dramatically improves the productivity of individuals and critical business processes.

Bandwidth Savings

WAN optimization can also bring tremendous savings in bandwidth costs. While the cost of bandwidth has been declining steadily in metropolitan North America and Europe, high speed links are still expensive in many parts of the world. Bandwidth availability can also be unreliable over satellite connections transmitting to offshore ships and remote locations like mines.

Through a combination of compression and de-duplication techniques, WAN optimization can significantly reduce the amount of bandwidth needed to transmit information across a link. Bandwidth reduction on the order of 60-95% is typical and this reduction in bandwidth directly translates into significant cost savings.

Consolidation

A dictionary definition of consolidation is *"the bringing together of businesses or business activities into a single unit."* With respect to IT, consolidation means the bringing together of servers and other IT infrastructure back to a centralized data center.

Why consolidate? Consolidation makes it easier to manage centralized resources as opposed to disparate resources scattered around the world. Companies may also not be able to staff skilled

IT personnel at every branch location. Consolidation enables companies to better leverage IT personnel at headquarters to manage IT for all locations.

Consolidation also simplifies the process of performing backups for the enterprise. With consolidation, backups can be performed at one central location instead of at many different branch locations around the world.

There is also the issue of security. It is not always easy to ensure the security of sensitive data stored in branch locations. By consolidating servers and storage to a centralized and secured data center, the job of making sure an enterprise's sensitive data is safe becomes much easier.

But consolidation introduces the problem of latency over the WAN. Because of latency, accessing centralized resources over long distances is often not practical or feasible. But by knocking down performance barriers and making the WAN "feel like a LAN", WAN optimization enables the consolidation of IT infrastructure.

Disaster Recovery and Replication

Preparing for possible disaster and catastrophic loss of data is an essential requirement of any IT organization. This means organizations must make sure that their data is backed up and secured at a remote location in the event of disaster.

Data is backed up to disk or to tape. When backing up to tape, the tape must physically be moved to a distant location in order to ensure its availability in the event of a site disaster. The process of backing up to tape can be tedious and prone to human error. Yet tape is still commonly used because it is relatively cheap compared to backing up to disk.

When backing up to disk, the backup data on disk is usually copied across the network to disks at a secondary site using data replication software. The process of backup and replication over the network is faster and simpler than backing up to tape. But it is also more expensive as it requires duplicate storage hardware at a secondary site as well as large amounts of available bandwidth. And depending on the volume of data and the backup window constraints, backup and replication over the WAN may not be feasible due to insufficient bandwidth and throughput.

WAN optimization makes the process of backing up over the network much faster and more cost efficient. By applying compression and de-duplication techniques, WAN optimization can significantly reduce bandwidth requirements on otherwise congested WAN links.

But there are times when limited bandwidth isn't the problem. In fact it's the opposite. Sometimes a high bandwidth link of 100Mbps or more has been dedicated for backup traffic but the backup solution fails to fully utilize the available bandwidth. The result is wasted bandwidth and smaller throughput. WAN optimization can help in these cases by maximizing the effective throughput and utilization of the WAN link for backup and replication traffic.

With WAN optimization, backing up and restoring data over the WAN becomes a much faster alternative to doing manual tape backups locally. It allows data sitting at the branch to be backed up directly to headquarters or to the secondary site within shorter backup windows.

Together, the "ABCDs" of WAN optimization deliver superior performance and reduced costs for IT infrastructure. Next, we explore the barriers to performance across the WAN and how WAN optimization overcomes these barriers.

Barriers to Performance across the WAN

Before going into the details of how WAN optimization works, we must first understand what the barriers are to application performance across the WAN.

Latency

Latency is time delay. This time delay can mean different things depending on what you are measuring. To the network engineer, latency can be the milliseconds it takes for a single packet to travel from a client machine to a server. To a web application user, latency can be the second it takes to get a response from a mouse click. And to the engineer working on a large CAD file from a remote file server, latency can be the minutes it takes to open the file.

High latency kills application performance. It can turn seconds into minutes when opening a large file or downloading email. It can also render a remote desktop session jittery and practically unusable.

It may seem intuitively obvious that latency should be greater across the WAN versus the LAN because of physical distance. But distance is only part of the problem when running applications across the WAN. Application latency across the WAN is caused by a combination of limited bandwidth and chatty protocols.

Limited Bandwidth

Limited bandwidth is a major barrier to performance over the WAN. Bandwidth is the measure of how much data can be transferred through a link over time and is usually measured in bits per second.

Bandwidth is usually not a problem on a LAN. Within an office bandwidth speeds of 100 megabits per second (Mbps) or more is common.

But across the WAN, bandwidth becomes much more expensive. Anyone with internet service knows that service providers charge more money for more bandwidth. Bandwidth over public networks must also be shared with potentially millions of other users. For this reason, limited bandwidth becomes a bottleneck to application performance across the WAN.

Transport Protocol Chattiness

The second barrier to performance is the chattiness of transport layer protocols. To be more specific, the chattiness of the TCP protocol hinders performance across the WAN.

The TCP protocol was designed with reliability, not performance in mind. TCP relies on a constant chatter of packets going back and forth in order to acknowledge the delivery and receipt of traffic. With this reliability comes a sacrifice in terms of performance.

Application Level Chattiness

Application protocols can be chatty as well. Take CIFS for example. CIFS is Microsoft's protocol for sharing files across a network. CIFS works by exchanging different types of messages back and forth between the client and the file server. Examples of these message types are open, read and close file. When a large file is read, hundreds or thousands of such request and response messages are sent back and forth between client and server. The file is read one section at a time. On a local network this back and forth chatter is usually tolerable but on a WAN it becomes magnified and grows into a huge barrier to performance. CIFS is probably the most common example of a chatty application protocol but many other common application protocols such as HTTP, Microsoft Exchange and NFS behave similarly.

8

READ

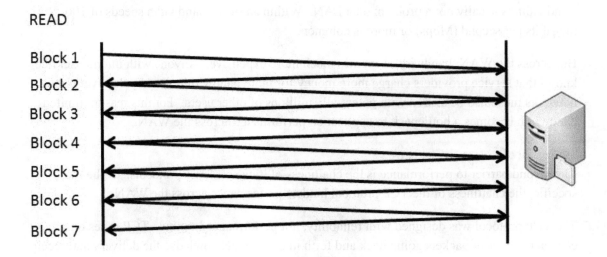

Figure 1-1 *Example of Chattiness in acknowledging blocks before requesting more*

Together, limited bandwidth and protocol chattiness are the primary barriers to application performance across the WAN. In the next section we dive into how Riverbed's SteelHead appliance product family can overcome these barriers to performance.

Summary

WAN optimization is a collection of techniques used to bring greater efficiencies in transferring data over wide area networks. These greater efficiencies bring tremendous benefits in the areas of application acceleration, bandwidth savings, consolidation and Disaster recovery and replication. Together these "ABCDs" of WAN optimization have dramatically changed the face of IT by helping companies deliver much better performance while reducing IT infrastructure costs.

Chapter 2: Riverbed Optimization System (RiOS)

Architecture

Overview

RiOS is the software that powers Riverbed SteelHead appliances. RiOS powers all of Riverbed's WAN optimization solutions including Riverbed® SteelHead ® Mobile software, Riverbed® SteelHead® Cloud Edition, and Riverbed® Virtual SteelHead® appliance. We focus on the SteelHead hardware appliance in this book.

RiOS is a symmetrical solution. It needs to be running on both ends of a WAN connection. SteelHead appliances running RiOS can be deployed on simple point to point, fully meshed or hub and spoke networks. As long as a SteelHead appliance is on both ends of a connection, the connection can be optimized.

When two SteelHead appliances are optimizing a connection, one appliance functions as the client side SteelHead appliance and the other as the server side SteelHead appliance. As the name suggests, the client side SteelHead appliance sits on the side where a connection is initiated from. It receives the initial TCP SYN packet from the client application.

The server side SteelHead appliance typically sits in the data center or head office close to where the servers are physically located. The server side SteelHead appliance receives TCP SYN packets and peers with the client side SteelHead appliance to optimize TCP connections.

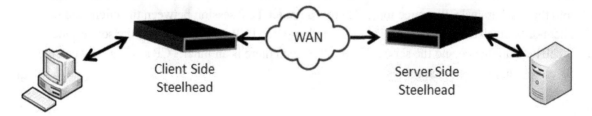

Figure 2-1 *Client and Server Side SteelHead appliance*

Auto Discovery

Auto discovery is a feature that enables a client and server side SteelHead appliance to automatically "discover" and peer with one another to optimize TCP connections. It is a feature that makes the SteelHead appliances easier to deploy. With Auto Discovery, there is no need to manually configure the peering of SteelHead appliances across the WAN.

How does auto discovery work? It works through the use of probes that are inserted into TCP packets. Whenever a client initiates a TCP connection to a server, it creates a TCP SYN packet. A client side SteelHead appliance that is in path will intercept this packet and insert a probe into the TCP SYN packet's header. Specifically, it marks the TCP options field with the hexadecimal value 0x4c (or 76 in decimal format). The TCP SYN packet with the probe travels across the WAN and is intercepted by the server side SteelHead appliance. When the server side SteelHead appliance sees the probe 0x4c it "discovers" the presence of a client side SteelHead appliance. The server side SteelHead appliance responds by sending a TCP SYN/ACK that includes the server side SteelHead appliance's IP address. Upon receipt of this special SYN/ACK, the client side SteelHead appliance "discovers" the server side SteelHead appliance.

Sometimes a third SteelHead appliance may be in the network path between the client and server side SteelHead appliances. To ensure that peering occurs between the outer SteelHead appliances only, RiOS also has a feature called Enhanced Auto Discovery which ensures that the outer SteelHead appliances at both ends discover each other. We describe the mechanism of how Enhanced Auto Discovery works in more detail in Chapter 5.

TCP Proxy

Once the SteelHead appliances auto-discover each other they can begin optimizing the TCP connection. When a connection is optimized, what was originally one TCP connection is split into three separate TCP connections. There's an outer TCP session between the client and the client-side SteelHead appliance. There is another outer TCP session between the server-side SteelHead appliance and the server. And in between there is an inner TCP session between the SteelHead appliances themselves.

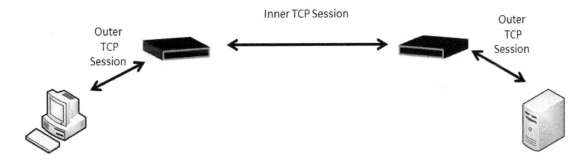

Figure 2-2 *SteelHead appliances function as TCP Proxy*

The inner session between the SteelHead appliances contains optimized traffic. Optimized traffic is generally compressed and de-duplicated. Note that the client's requests are transparently served by the client-side SteelHead appliance. The server side SteelHead appliance makes requests to the actual server on the client's behalf. For this reason, the SteelHead appliances function as a TCP proxy for optimized traffic. Non-optimized traffic (such as Internet traffic and traffic destined to locations without SteelHead appliances) is passed through the SteelHead appliances unaltered.

Correct Addressing

The SteelHead appliances by default use a WAN visibility mode called correct addressing for their inner TCP connection over the WAN. In correct addressing, the source and destination IP address of packets between the SteelHead appliances is that of the SteelHead appliances and not of the original client and server. In other words, the SteelHead appliances perform a network address translation from the original source and destination IP addresses to the SteelHead appliance's IP addresses. The destination IP port used on the server side SteelHead appliance for inner TCP connections is 7800.

12

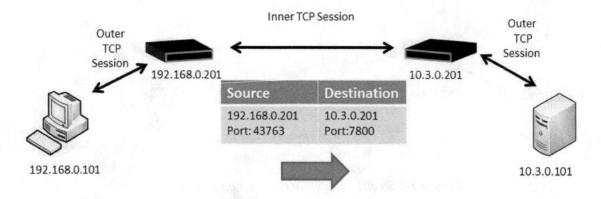

Figure 2-3 *Correct Addressing*

Correct addressing is one of several different WAN visibility modes that the SteelHead appliances can use. In addition to correct addressing, the SteelHeads can use other WAN visibility modes that preserve the original client and server IP addresses and ports in packets going across the WAN. Making these original addresses and ports visible across the WAN is sometimes necessary when working with a firewall or QoS device. We describe the different WAN visibility modes in more detail in chapter 5.

Streamlining Techniques

RiOS employs multiple techniques for optimizing WAN traffic. These techniques can be grouped into what are called three categories of "streamlining" techniques:

- Data Streamlining
- Transport Streamlining
- Application Streamlining

Data Streamlining focuses on reducing the amount of data flowing across the network. Transport Streamlining focuses on making the TCP protocol more efficient. Application Streamlining uses techniques specific to application protocols to reduce latency. Together, these three classes of streamlining techniques provide a comprehensive and multi-layer approach to streamlining and optimizing the flow of data across the WAN.

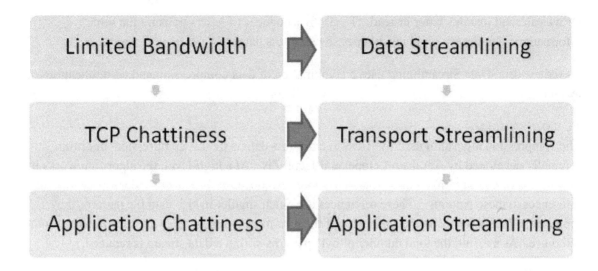

Figure 2-4 *RiOS Streamlining Techniques*

It is important to note that the three streamlining techniques operate independently of each other at different layers of the network stack. This means that if one of the techniques doesn't work in a certain environment the other two can continue to optimize traffic. For example, sometimes RiOS will encounter a custom application that RiOS does not understand and cannot perform application streamlining. But as long as the underlying transport protocol is TCP/IP, RiOS can continue to perform data and transport streamlining. RiOS is a true multi-layer optimization solution.

We now discuss each of these three streamlining techniques in more detail.

Data Streamlining

Data Streamlining uses a combination of data compression and de-duplication techniques to reduce the amount of data flowing across the WAN. In doing so, it reduces network bandwidth usage and costs. Before proceeding it is important to first distinguish the subtle but important difference between "data" and "information." Data going across the network is raw unorganized byte patterns of 1's and 0's. Information is data that has been processed and organized to make it useful. The goal of Data Streamlining is to enable the transmission of useful information using the least amount of data as possible. Data Streamlining enables applications to exchange the same amount of useful information using much less data. Here's a simple analogy. If we want to transmit the result of a coin toss, we can do so by sending across the following letters: TAILS.

Or we can send just this letter instead: 'T'. Both sequences of letters transmit the same information. But the latter obviously does so using less data.

To reduce data, Data Streamlining uses a combination of data compression and de-duplication techniques.

LZ Compression

The compression algorithm used by RiOS to compress data is the LZ compression algorithm originally developed by Abraham Lempel and Jacob Ziv. At a high-level, the algorithm works by finding sequential patterns of data that occur more than once. It then builds a dictionary of references to these patterns. These references are much smaller in size than the patterns they represent. When subsequent occurrences of the data pattern appear, they are substituted with the reference. As a result, the total number of byte patterns within a data stream is reduced.

RiOS will apply LZ compression whenever it sees unique data for the first time or during what is called a "cold read." The amount of data reduction achieved through LZ compression varies with the data type. LZ compression in most cases will provide a modest bandwidth improvement in performance during an initial cold read. Scalable Data Referencing is used to achieve even greater data reduction and performance.

Scalable Data Referencing (SDR)

Scalable Data Referencing or SDR is the name of the technique RiOS uses for data de-duplication. SDR works by replacing duplicate byte patterns within TCP data streams with references when sent over the WAN. These references point to the original data which is stored in a special data dictionary called the data store. When SDR is applied to data going across a link, what actually goes across is a combination of compressed new byte patterns and references to byte patterns stored in the data store.

SDR vs. LZ Compression

Like LZ compression, SDR reduces data by substituting redundant byte patterns with much smaller dictionary references. But while LZ compression eliminates redundancy within a single data stream, SDR eliminates redundancy across multiple data streams and can reference further back in time e.g., previous TCP sessions. And since files are made up of multiple data streams, this can make a huge difference when transferring multiple files with common data. Rather than trying to compress and find redundancies within a single file each time, a single large file that is hundreds of megabytes in size can be reduced down to a tiny reference of just a few bytes through SDR.

Because it eliminates redundancy across multiple TCP data streams, SDR typically achieves much higher rates of data reduction than LZ compression. When combined with LZ compression, SDR can typically reduce the amount of data transferred across WAN links by 60-95%.

SDR Data Dictionary

In order for SDR to work, a common dictionary of byte patterns needs to be built on both ends of the WAN link. This is where the SteelHead appliances come in. Every SteelHead appliance has dedicated storage called the data store for storing the SDR data dictionary. This dictionary stores byte patterns and references to these patterns. These byte patterns usually range from 8 to 512 bytes in size and average about 128 bytes. The references themselves are much smaller ranging up to 13 bytes. By using variable block sizes (as opposed to fixed block sizes) SDR is very efficient at finding redundant byte patterns resulting in better data reduction.

For even greater data reduction efficiencies, references can refer to other references in a hierarchical fashion. SDR uses up to four layers of referencing. Using this technique, it is possible to have an entire file hundreds of megabytes or more in size referenced by a single 128 byte pattern.

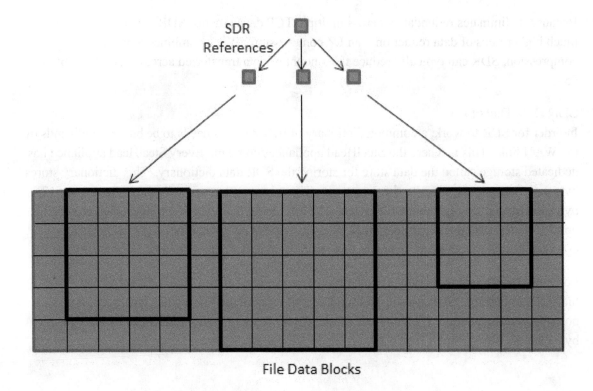

SDR
References

File Data Blocks

Figure 2-5 *SDR Pyramid –Tiny SDR references refer to variable sized data blocks in a file*

Universal Data Store

SteelHead appliances use a universal data store as opposed to a per peer data store. A universal data store will store each unique byte pattern that is used by multiple peer appliances just once. In contrast, a per peer data store will store a copy of each unique byte pattern for each peer. The advantage of using a universal data store is that it makes data center appliances serving multiple sites much more scalable.

Each SteelHead appliances come with a finite data store ranging in size from 40 GB to over 4 TB. In the event the data store becomes full, existing data segments are purged in order to make room for new segments. A Least Recently Used (LRU) algorithm is used by default to delete segments from a data store that has reached full capacity.

Building the SDR Dictionary

How is the SDR dictionary on the data store built? It is built whenever a TCP stream with new data is transferred across a link that has a SteelHead appliance on both ends. Remember, files are made up of one or more TCP streams. So when a file is transferred across, the first SteelHead appliance on the link will inspect and break the TCP streams that make up the file into unique byte patterns. If it finds a byte pattern that is new it will create a unique dictionary reference for that pattern and share the reference and the pattern with the SteelHead appliance on the other end of the link. These dictionary references and byte pattern pairs are kept on the data store on both SteelHead appliances.

If instead of a new byte pattern, RiOS finds a byte pattern that already exist on both data stores, the SteelHead appliance will transfer the tiny reference instead of the entire byte pattern across the WAN. The SteelHead appliance on the other side can then lookup the reference in its own data store to find the byte pattern and replace the reference with it.

Since RiOS examines data at the byte level, files that have changed can still be transferred across very fast in de-duplicated form. RiOS can find the byte patterns that are new and transfer them across along with references to the patterns in the file that have not changed. This works especially well for text based data found in word processing documents and spreadsheets. Data reduction on the order of 90% or more is not uncommon for these types of files.

The process of building and looking up SDR references to gigabytes of data at almost wire speed is made possible by the use of high-end computing on both ends. The SteelHead appliances are essentially super computers performing incredibly high rates of pattern matching, hashing and lookups on network traffic.

SDR is the core Data Streamlining technique for improving performance in RiOS. But on top of SDR, RiOS also provides Transport and Application Streamlining techniques for improving performance.

Transport Streamlining

Transport Streamlining addresses the inefficiencies that exist in the transport protocol layer. Specifically, it streamlines TCP.

TCP was designed with reliability in mind, not performance. To ensure reliability, TCP relies on acknowledgements from the receiver before more packets can be sent across the link. This constant chatter of packets going back and forth results in higher latency for applications running across the wide area network.

Virtual Window Expansion

How does RiOS address the chattiness of TCP? By reducing the total number of roundtrips needed. RiOS does this by "packing" more information that is sent across with each packet. By packing more information in each payload the total number of roundtrips needed is reduced. This process is called Virtual Windows Expansion.

This leads to another question. How exactly does RiOS "pack" more information in each TCP packet? Through the use of dictionary references that reference larger data. The same references used in SDR are used to fill TCP packets. Since a tiny reference can represent much larger amounts of data this is how a TCP window can be virtually expanded and effectively carry the same amount of information fewer bytes of data.

High-Speed and Max-TCP

High-Speed and Max-TCP are two features designed to increase and maximize the throughput of TCP traffic. So far we have discussed how RiOS can reduce bandwidth usage. But sometimes it is preferable to *maximize* bandwidth utilization and thus throughput instead. This may be the case if the data being transferred isn't very compressible but plenty of bandwidth is available. A company might have what can be called a "Long Fat Network." A Long Fat Network is a network link that has both high latency and high bandwidth.

With "Long Fat Networks", bandwidth is often *underutilized* because of the way TCP behaves. Under normal circumstances, TCP will maintain its window size as long as packets are being acknowledged. However, if there are unacknowledged packets and packet loss is detected, TCP assumes that there is congestion and enters into congestion avoidance mode. The window size is cut in half causing available bandwidth to be underutilized.

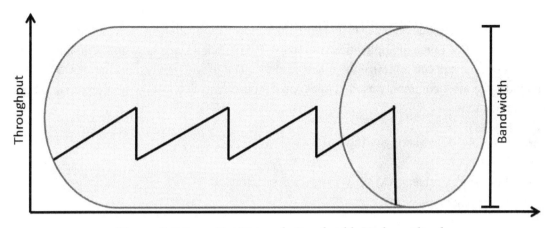

Figure 2-6 *Long Fat Network, Bandwidth Under-utilized*

High-Speed and Max-TCP are two features in RiOS that address the problem of underutilized links. They work by having the SteelHead appliance continually and aggressively "blast" packets through the pipe even in the event of detected packet loss.

The difference between High-Speed and Max TCP is that High-Speed TCP is designed to back off *slowly* in the event that packet loss is detected. Max-TCP on the other hand does not back off at all. Hence, Max-TCP is more aggressive. Because it is more aggressive, the downside of using Max versus High-Speed TCP is that Max TCP traffic can "starve" out other competing traffic on the link.

High Speed and Max-TCP are commonly used in backup and replication scenarios where there is plenty of bandwidth dedicated. These features can also be used to maximize bandwidth utilization on links suffering from excessive packet loss.

Connection Pooling

RiOS also streamlines TCP through the use of connection pooling. In connection pooling, the SteelHead appliance opens and maintains a set of TCP connections with its peer appliance across the WAN before it is actually needed. The default number of connections in the pool is 20. New client requests across the WAN can then use these already open connections without going through the TCP handshake process. This saves on the overhead needed each time a TCP connection is setup. Connection Pooling is especially useful for saving time on short-lived TCP connections.

Application Streamlining

One of RiOS's biggest advantages is its ability to perform application specific optimization methods for a wide range of application protocols. RiOS understands how different applications protocols behave and can optimize them accordingly. The list of applications that RiOS is aware of includes the most commonly used applications in business. The following is a partial list of these applications:

- Windows File Sharing (CIFS)
- Web (HTTP)
- Microsoft Exchange (MAPI)
- Lotus Notes
- FTP

The collection of techniques used to accelerate these applications is called application streamlining.

Transaction Prediction

The core technique in application streamlining is called Transaction Prediction. Transaction Prediction is the ability to predict and perform application level operations ahead of time. For example, if the server side SteelHead appliance sees a request to read block number one in a file, it can predict with great probability that more requests are coming to read blocks two, three, four and so on. Rather than wait for all of these requests to arrive one by one from across the WAN, the server-side SteelHead appliance can go ahead and read the subsequent blocks and pipeline the data across the WAN. When the requests to read subsequent blocks finally do come, they can be fulfilled by the client side SteelHead appliance. Extra roundtrips across the WAN are avoided.

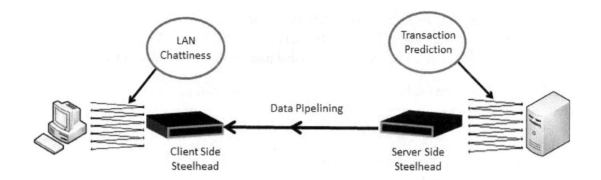

Figure 2-7 *Application Streamlining*

The ability to perform Transaction Prediction behavior depends of course on an understanding of how different application protocols work. Fortunately, most operations on a computer are very predictable and repetitive. The same goes for application protocols such as CIFS, NFS, HTTP and so on. This makes it possible for RiOS to predict with great probability which block in a file to read next after an initial request.

Application Modules

In addition to Transaction Prediction, RiOS has application modules that can perform additional optimization techniques specific to an application protocol. We devote the remainder of this chapter to describing these application modules in RIOS.

CIFS

CIFS (also known as Server Message Block or SMB) is Microsoft's protocol for sharing files over the network. It runs over TCP port 445. SMB was originally developed at IBM in the 1980s and then renamed the Common Internet File System by Microsoft in the 1990s.

CIFS was developed for accessing files across a local network. It is a very chatty protocol and was not designed with the WAN in mind. Hence, the performance penalties that come with a chatty protocol become magnified across the WAN resulting in much slower response times for basic file. Anyone who has tried opening or copying a very large Word or Excel file across the WAN can attest to this.

Fortunately, the messages that make up the CIFS protocol are well documented. CIFS protocol behavior is generally very repetitive and predictable. RiOS can apply Transaction Prediction to CIFS and mitigate the effects of latency when accessing files over the network.

With RiOS, CIFS performance across the WAN can be improved dramatically. Performance increases on the order of 25 times is typical. If a very large CAD file is taking 25 minutes to transfer across the WAN, RiOS can usually bring that transfer time down to about a minute.

In addition to Transaction Prediction, RiOS provides additional optimization features specific to CIFS.

SMB Signing

SMB Signing is a feature for digitally signing SMB packets to ensure that they have not been altered by a "man in the middle" attack. SMB signing is usually required when accessing file shares on a Windows domain controller.

Since the SteelHead appliance is essentially a "man in the middle" between the client and file server, SMB signing could prevent the SteelHead appliance from performing transaction prediction. Transaction prediction requires that the server side SteelHead appliance be able to perform its own read-ahead operations on the back end file server on behalf of the original client. But SMB signing prevents anyone besides original client from performing such operations.

RiOS provides a mechanism for performing transaction prediction even when SMB signing is enabled between the client and file server. This mechanism requires that the server side SteelHead appliance join and become a member of the Windows active directory domain. This will allow the server side SteelHead appliance to obtain the cryptographic keys it needs in order to establish an SMB signed connection with the file server. We describe the steps for implementing this mechanism for optimizing SMB signed connections in detail in chapter 5.

Overlapping Open Optimization

Overlapping Open Optimization is a technique that provides better performance for applications which repeatedly open and close the same file. CAD applications are a good example of an application that exhibits this "Overlapping Open" behavior. The act of opening and closing a file repeatedly can hinder performance as the client needs to obtain and release an opportunistic lock (or "Oplock") over and over again. In addition, RiOS cannot fully optimize CIFS traffic if an Oplock is not available because it would not be safe.

The Overlapping Open Optimization feature addresses this by having the server side SteelHead appliance obtain and maintain an exclusive Oplock on behalf of the client. Having the server side SteelHead appliance maintain an Oplock allows for full optimization of CIFS applications with overlapping opens.

It is important to remember that when the SteelHead appliance obtains an Oplock, all file access must go through the SteelHead appliance. A local user on the file server will not be able to read/write to the file.

Applock Optimization

Applock Optimization is a technique that improves the performance of reading and writing to Word and Excel files. It is similar to Overlapping Open Optimization in that the server side SteelHead appliance obtains and maintains a lock on a file on behalf of the client. It differs in that this lock is obtained at the application level versus the file level.

Print Optimization

RiOS can also perform Print Optimization to optimize print traffic from the branch office to a central print server at the data center.

SMBv2

In 2006 Microsoft released SMB version 2 as an update to the SMB protocol. Microsoft operating systems using Windows Vista or later now use SMBv2 by default. However, newer operating systems such as Windows 2008 can negotiate back to using SMBv1 with older peers using SMBv1.

SMBv2 was designed to be less chatty that its predecessor. In SMBv2 the number of commands is reduced from over a hundred to nineteen. RiOS can apply Transaction Prediction techniques on SMBv2 commands, just as it can with SMBv1, to reduce roundtrips and latency. These techniques include read-ahead, write-behind, and the caching of file attributes and directory content. Hence, while SMBv2 alone can deliver better performance across the WAN than SMB1, the performance of optimized SMBv2 traffic with RiOS is even better.

RiOS also gives you the option to down negotiate SMBv2 connections to SMB1. However, an optimized SMBv2 connection will generally perform better than an optimized SMB1 connection.

CIFS Prepopulation

The CIFS Prepopulation feature allows you to specify CIFS file shares to be read by the SteelHead appliances in advance. By reading or "pre-populating" the SteelHead appliance data stores in advance, end users can avoid feeling the effects of latency or building the data store when accessing files for the first time.

RiOS 7 allows you to create flexible policies for CIFS Prepopulation. You can prepopulate based on when files were created, modified or last accessed. You can also prepopulate files matching a certain size or regular expression.

HTTP

The Hypertext Transfer Protocol initially was used just to transfer text based messages on the World Wide Web. It is now used by web browsers to access web pages and applications. Examples of popular web applications from the business world include Microsoft SharePoint, Oracle Forms and Lotus Notes.

In the early days of the web, most web applications were nothing more than static pages of text. Modern web applications are now rich with multimedia content. But the underlying HTTP protocol retrieves the different objects making up this content separately resulting in inefficiencies over the WAN.

RiOS includes optimization techniques geared towards accelerating and improving the user experience with web applications. These techniques fall into three main categories: Basic Tuning, Prefetch Schemes and Authentication Tuning.

Auto Configuration

There are many options for tuning and configuring HTTP optimization. It may not always be obvious which of the settings need to be configured. To address this, RiOS 7.0 introduced the Auto Configuration feature for HTTP optimization. With Auto Configuration, the SteelHead appliance can automatically configure the optimal settings for HTTP optimization. Auto Configuration works by having the SteelHead appliances collect statistics on a per-web server basis and adjust the HTTP settings on the client side SteelHead appliance accordingly.

Manual Configuration

Auto Configuration makes the job of enabling HTTP optimization much simpler. But HTTP optimization settings can also be configured manually. We now describe the different options for configuring HTTP optimization.

Strip Compression

In Strip Compression, the SteelHead appliance disables normal compression between the web browser and the server. Since the SteelHead appliance's SDR technique is far effective in delivering data reduction, disabling the native compression and replacing it with SDR will usually deliver much better data reduction results.

Insert Cookie

Sometimes an HTTP application does not use cookies. The Insert Cookie feature allows the SteelHead appliance to insert its own cookie so that it can track individual user sessions.

Insert Keep Alive

Insert Keep Alive enables the server side SteelHead appliance to keep alive an existing HTTP connection with the web server even if the client has closed the connection. By keeping the connection alive, the SteelHead appliance can continue to use the connection to pre-fetch other objects.

Prefetch Schemes

URL Learning

In URL Learning, RiOS is able to learn the association between base URL requests and follow on requests. For example, if the SteelHead appliance sees an http GET request for the object "mypicture.jpg" it will note that the Referer in the request is "http://mywebsite." RiOS will build an association between the two objects so the next time it sees a request for http://mywebsite it will be able to pre-fetch the associated objects such as "mypicture.jpg." The server side SteelHead appliance can then pipeline and send the object(s) to the client side SteelHead appliance immediately and reduce the number of roundtrips across the WAN. URL Learning works best for static web pages where the content does not change.

Parse & Prefetch

While URL Learning works well with static web pages, the Parse & Prefetch optimization feature works well with dynamic web pages. In Parse & Prefetch, the server side SteelHead appliance will parse an HTML page and look inside the HTLM tags for objects such as image files and style sheets that can be pre-fetched. Instead of waiting for the HTTP client to send these requests, the server side SteelHead appliance will go ahead and pre-fetch these objects and send to the client side SteelHead appliance. When the HTTP client finally does issue the request for these objects, the client side SteelHead appliance will be able to fulfill the request without the need for extra roundtrips across the WAN.

Object Prefetch Table

The Object Prefetch Table allows the client side SteelHead appliance to cache web objects so that they only need to be fetched once across the WAN. Examples of web objects include images, JavaScript files and cascading style sheets.

Authentication Tuning

In addition to Basic Tuning and Prefetch Schemes, RiOS can also optimize the methods used to authenticate the web client.

Reuse Auth

Web browsers will frequently open parallel connections to download objects faster. The Reuse Auth feature will "reuse" the authentication of a base connection and allow additional connections from the same session to access pre-fetched objects from the client side SteelHead appliance. This feature works if the server is using NTLM or Kerberos as its authentication method.

Force NTLM

The Force NTLM feature "forces" the web browser and server to use NTLM instead of Kerberos as the authentication method. Kerberos is less efficient over the WAN because it requires each request to be authenticated as well as communication with the domain controller.

Strip Auth Header

The Strip Auth Header feature will strip the authentication header information inside an HTTP request if it is part of an already authenticated connection. That way the request does not have to go through the authentication process again.

Gratuitous 401

An HTTP server will return status code 401 if authentication has failed. When per-request authentication is required, multiple 401 codes can get sent back across the WAN. In such cases, the Gratuitous 401 feature can have the client side SteelHead appliance cache the response and return status 401 locally without additional roundtrips across the WAN.

Oracle Forms

Oracle Forms is a platform that allows business applications such as Oracle's EBusiness Suite to access a backend Oracle database. It uses a Java based applet in the browser that communicates with the database. This Java based applet runs in a Java Virtual Machine environment that was originally called "JInitiator." But after Oracle's acquisition of SUN Microsystems in 2009, it was renamed SUN JVM.

The challenge of optimizing this traffic from JInitiator/SUN JVM is that it is encrypted. RiOS is able to apply Data and Transport Streamlining to this encrypted traffic by transparently decrypting, optimizing and re-encrypting the traffic. It is important to note that RiOS does not apply any application streamlining techniques specific to Oracle Forms traffic. Hence, while significant bandwidth reduction can be achieved with RiOS, the end user sometimes may not feel significant latency reduction. Thus this is most useful for networks with low latency and low bandwidth, rather than high latency.

MAPI

The Messaging Application Programming Interface (MAPI) is an API from Microsoft for exchanging email messages between email client programs and servers. Outlook clients use MAPI to send and receive email messages with Exchange servers.

RiOS can perform Transaction Prediction on Read, Write and Sync operations for MAPI. MAPI optimization is especially useful when sending large attachments to multiple recipients as RiOS makes sure that unique data in the attachments is sent across the WAN just once.

Outlook Anywhere

Outlook Anywhere allows Outlook clients to access their Exchange server from outside the corporate network or VPN using RPC over HTTP(s). Prior to RiOS 6.5, SteelHead appliances could perform Data and Transport Streamlining but not Application Streamlining on Outlook Anywhere traffic. RiOS 6.5 and higher provides full latency optimization at the application layer for Outlook Anywhere traffic.

Encrypted MAPI

Microsoft Exchange encrypts MAPI traffic by default. SteelHead appliances can be configured to optimize encrypted MAPI traffic provided that the server side SteelHead appliance joins the Windows domain. Steps on how to configure optimization for encrypted MAPI are described in more detail in chapter 5.

Transparent Prepopulation

The Transparent Prepopulation feature for MAPI allows the SteelHead appliances to continue downloading new email to the client side SteelHead appliance even if the Outlook client is offline. Once the Outlook client comes back online, the client side SteelHead appliance can deliver new email without additional roundtrips across the WAN.

Transparent Prepopulation uses virtual connections between the client side SteelHead appliance and the Exchange server. When an existing connection between the Outlook client and the Exchange server goes offline, the client side SteelHead appliance creates a virtual connection with the Exchange server and uses it to pull over new email across the WAN and prepopulate the client side SteelHead appliance. If a new Outlook connection for the user is identified, this virtual connection terminates.

MS-SQL

MS SQL uses the Tabular Data Stream (TDS) protocol to transfer data between the SQL database server and a client. TDS is one of the few major business protocols which RiOS cannot automatically optimize using application streamlining techniques.

Starting with MS SQL Server 2005, Microsoft began encrypting a key packet, the TDS login packet inside SQL that RiOS needs to be able to read in order to perform Transaction Prediction. Hence, while RiOS can still apply Data and Transport Streamlining and achieve significant data reduction, it is often hit or miss as to whether it can achieve significant improvement in SQL application response times.

For customers needing optimization of MS SQL applications, Riverbed recommends gathering traces of the application SQL traffic and sending it to Riverbed Professional Services. From there, Riverbed can determine if any additional tuning of the MS SQL module can improve the application performance.

NFS

The Network File System protocol allows clients to access files across a network. It was originally developed by SUN Microsystems in 1984 and is primarily used in UNIX and Linux environments. Like CIFS, NFS was originally intended for file access across a local network and is a very chatty protocol.

The original NFS protocol version 1 was developed to use UDP as its transport mechanism over the network and cannot be optimized by RiOS. NFS versions 2, 3 and 4 use TCP instead of UDP. However, RiOS can provide full optimization at the data, transport and application layers for NFS version 3 only. For NFS versions 2 and 4, RiOS can perform data reduction but no application level latency reduction.

Lotus Notes

Lotus Notes is IBM's client-server software platform for email, messaging, calendar and collaboration. Lotus Notes Client programs communicate with an application server called Lotus Domino.

RiOS can perform both data reduction as well as latency optimization on Lotus Notes traffic even if it is compressed. Lotus Notes can use either Huffman or LZ compression to reduce the size of email attachments. RiOS can perform data reduction on such compressed attachments by decompressing, optimizing and re-compressing the data after it is sent across the WAN.

RiOS also has a mechanism for optimizing encrypted Lotus Notes traffic. This mechanism requires importing the server ID file from the Lotus Domino server into the server side SteelHead appliance. With the server ID file, the SteelHead appliance can act as the Domino server and authenticate an encrypted connection while establishing an un-encrypted connection with the actual Domino server.

Citrix ICA

Independent Computing Architecture (ICA) is a proprietary protocol from Citrix for passing data between a client and a server. It is used by Citrix's popular virtual desktop solution XenApp (formerly Presentation Server) to transmit user interface information such as keystrokes, mouse movements, screen updates and so on between the XenApp server and a remote user.

The user experience of ICA over the WAN can vary widely depending on the latency and available bandwidth. RiOS has the ability to automatically disable native Citrix compression of ICA traffic and apply much more efficient methods of data reduction. Bandwidth reduction of ICA traffic is typically in the range of 40-60%. RiOS though its data reduction methods for ICA can turn an "un-useable" experience caused by limited bandwidth into a much more useable LAN like experience. It can also allow more users to be added to an office without requiring a network upgrade.

ICA over SSL

Sometimes ICA traffic is tunneled through SSL in order to provide a secure connection over a VPN to Citrix's Access Gateway appliance. RiOS can optimize ICA over SSL provided that the SSL certificate and key from the Access Gateway appliance is imported into the server side SteelHead appliance.

Client Drive Mapping

Citrix's Client Drive Mapping feature allows a user in an ICA session to map a drive on the Citrix server back to their own client machine. For example, a drive on the Citrix server can show up as C:\on the client. CDM allows users to save files back to their own drive rather than to the central server. Prior to RiOS 7.0, SteelHead appliances could only perform data reduction but no latency optimization on CDM traffic. With RIOS 7.0 and higher, SteelHead appliances can provide full application level latency optimization for CDM traffic as well.

Disaster Recovery

The term Disaster Recovery (DR) refers to IT processes for ensuring business continuity in the event of a disaster. It includes processes for backing up, replicating and restoring a company's critical data. Since DR must protect against potential loss of data at an entire site, it must naturally provide for the backing up and the restoring of data across long distances to and from a secondary location.

Backing up data over the WAN may seem like a simple approach for implementing DR. But limited bandwidth combined with latency and the large scale data transfers required by DR present huge performance barriers. The process of backing up and restoring large volumes of data over the WAN is often too slow to meet the narrow backup and recovery time windows companies require.

Behavioral Traffic Recognition

WAN optimization provides techniques for making backup and replication over the WAN possible. However there are some important differences when optimizing DR traffic as opposed to application traffic. Instead of being transactional and chatty, DR traffic tends to be high-rate and high-volume. The goal is to push as much data through in the shortest amount of time. To address this, RiOS utilizes a special application layer algorithm called Behavioral Traffic Recognition for DR traffic. This algorithm can identify large scale data transfers found in DR traffic and apply specific optimization methods for maximizing data throughput.

High-Speed & Max-TCP

Another challenge of backing up data over the WAN is bandwidth under-utilization. We have discussed earlier how an important benefit of WAN optimization is bandwidth reduction. But sometimes in the case of DR, the goal is to *increase* rather than decrease the utilization of available bandwidth. This is especially true when a high latency and high bandwidth connection (otherwise known as a "long fat network") has been dedicated for DR traffic. This is because standard TCP cannot take advantage of high bandwidth links due to the way it responds to unacknowledged or dropped packets. When a packet is unacknowledged or dropped, standard TCP will respond by cutting the TCP congestion window in half and thereby reducing the effective throughput. To address this, the Transport Streamlining methods of High Speed and Max TCP described earlier in this chapter can be enabled to maximize the throughput of DR traffic through long fat networks.

SDR-M

SDR-M is memory based de-duplication. Normal SDR uses disk-based de-duplication. SDR-M uses RAM memory only to build the data dictionary for SDR. This can result in better performance by avoiding the latency penalties of reading and writing to disk. SDR-M is the recommended setting in SAN replication scenarios using larger (non-SSD) SteelHead appliance models that have more RAM.

SDR-Adaptive

SDR-Adaptive uses a mix of disk based and memory based de-duplication. In SDR-Adaptive, RiOS monitors disk I/O response times as well as WAN utilization to select the optimal mix of disk and memory based de-duplication.

Summary

RiOS is the software that powers SteelHead appliances. RiOS needs to be running on both ends of a WAN link in order to optimize the connection. The techniques used by RiOS can be grouped into three types: Data Streamlining, Transport Streamlining and Application Streamlining. These three types of streamlining techniques operate at different layers of the network stack making RiOS a comprehensive multi-layer WAN optimization solution.

Chapter 3: The SteelHead Product Family

This chapter covers the different SteelHead WAN Optimization appliances from Riverbed. Since its initial introduction in 2004, SteelHead appliances have continued to evolve along with wide area networks. While the form factor and deployment models of different SteelHeads may differ, the underlying RiOS software running on all of these appliances remain fundamentally the same.

This chapter covers the concepts behind each type of SteelHead appliance. Step by step instructions for deploying the SteelHead appliance are covered in chapter 5.

SteelHead CX

The SteelHead CX appliance was first introduced in 2012 and remains the leading WAN optimization product in the market today. When first introduced, the SteelHead CX was dedicated to just one main function- WAN Optimization. But beginning in 2017, newer SteelHead CX appliances began to ship as "SteelHead SD Ready." The "SD Ready" refers to the fact that these appliances come shipped with the necessary memory and storage hardware requirements for delivering both WAN Optimization and SD-WAN features. SD-WAN features enable the SteelHead to dynamically steer traffic across multiple WAN links. (A complete discussion of SD-WAN is beyond the scope of this book.)

Each SteelHead CX appliance can be licensed as an 'L,' 'M' or 'H' model. (For Low, Medium or High) An 'L' SteelHead CX appliance model can be upgraded to an 'M' or 'H' model via license key to increase the Optimized WAN Capacity and Connection Count. We discuss SteelHead sizing in more detail in chapter 5. For up to date specifications of each SteelHead appliance model, please download the SteelHead appliance Spec Sheet at www.riverbed.com.

SteelHead SaaS

Overview

SteelHead SaaS delivers WAN optimization for popular Software as a Service (SaaS) applications. As of this writing, popular SaaS applications supported by SteelHead SaaS include:

- Box
- Microsoft Dynamics CRM

- Office 365
- Salesforce.com
- SuccessFactors
- ServiceNow
- Veeva

Remember that SteelHead WAN Optimization requires one or more client side SteelHeads connecting to at least one server side SteelHead. But how to deploy a server side SteelHead in a public SaaS provider's datacenter? The solution is to deploy a virtual instance of the SteelHead appliance "in the cloud" that is located in close physical proximity to the SaaS provider's datacenter. The cloud infrastructure that hosts a server side appliance for SteelHead SaaS is a point of presence (POP) owned and managed by Akamai Technologies.

Akamai Technology's cloud infrastructure hosts the server side SteelHead appliances in the cloud. Configuration of the SteelHead SaaS solution is performed from the Riverbed Cloud Portal.

SteelHead appliances running newer versions of RiOS (version 8.x and later) are all capable of optimizing traffic to SaaS applications. It does this by maintaining a list of destination IPs that map to the destination servers of major SaaS providers. When the client side SteelHead sees traffic destined for a SaaS application, it will redirect the traffic to an Akamai Edge Server. This traffic is encapsulated in UDP over port 9545. From there, the Akamai Edge Server will use Akamai's SureRoute technology to find the most optimal path within the Akamai overlay network to the SaaS destination. The traffic will then be routed to an Akamai server located in close physical proximity to the SaaS provider's server. It is on this server that a virtual instance of the SteelHead appliance called the Akamai Cloud SteelHead (ACSH) can be spun up to peer with the client side SteelHead as the server side SteelHead.

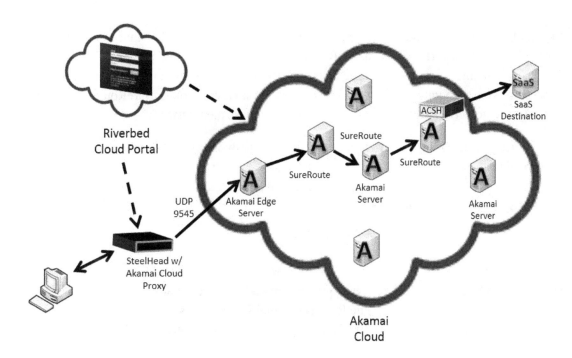

Figure 3-2 *SteelHead SaaS*

That's the high level description of how SteelHead SaaS works. Let's dive into more details of each component of the solution.

Akamai Cloud Proxy (ACP)

The Akamai Cloud Proxy (ACP) is software that runs on a client side SteelHead appliance. It is included on the most recent versions of RiOS. (Versions 8.x and later) The ACP is responsible for intercepting traffic destined to SaaS servers and redirecting the traffic to an Akamai Edge Server.

Akamai Cloud SteelHead (ACSH)

The Akamai Cloud SteelHead (ACSH) is a virtual instance of the SteelHead appliance that is launched on an Akamai server located in close proximity to the SaaS destination. The ACSH functions as the server side SteelHead in optimizing connections to a SaaS platform. Unlike with the client side SteelHead, there is no direct access available to manage or configure the ACSH.

SureRoute

Akamai has over a thousand physical servers located in over a hundred countries around the world. SureRoute leverages this vast network of servers to mitigate the effects of latency in delivering dynamic content across long distances. It does this by continually sending probes between servers to monitor latency and packet loss. From these probes, SureRoute can calculate the fastest route between any two Points of Presence across their network.

Hence, once SteelHead SaaS traffic enters the Akamai network on an Edge Server, it can be forwarded to an Akamai Gateway server over the best path. It travels along an overlay network that is calculated by SureRoute. For more details on Akamai's SureRoute technology, refer to Akamai's Developer website:

https://developer.akamai.com/learn/Optimization/SureRoute.html

Cloud Portal

SteelHead SaaS customers have access to the Riverbed Cloud Portal at https://cloudportal.riverbed.com. The Riverbed Cloud Portal serves two important functions: 1) SteelHead Appliance Registration and 2) Managing Proxy Certificates for SSL.

Appliance Registration

Before the Akamai Cloud Proxy software can intercept and forward any traffic to the cloud, the SteelHead appliance it is running on must first be registered to perform WAN Optimization for particular SaaS applications. Riverbed Cloud Portal is where SteelHead SaaS administrators can register on premise SteelHead appliances used for SaaS optimization. Every SteelHead SaaS customer has a unique Appliance Registration Key which they can retrieve from their Cloud Portal account. This Registration Key is then entered on each SteelHead appliance to register the appliance with the Cloud Portal. Once registered, the Cloud Portal can verify that a SteelHead appliance has the valid licensing and software to perform SaaS optimization.

Managing Proxy Certificates

The Riverbed Cloud Portal is also used for managing Proxy Certificates. Proxy Certificates for SSL are used to ensure a trusted and secure key exchange is executed for encrypting traffic over the public Internet. Before discussing Proxy Certificates further, let's first review how SSL works.

SaaS applications optimized by Riverbed are secured over the Internet using SSL. Whenever a client end user tries to access a SaaS application, the server will present a public key certificate that must be trusted by the client if the connection is to be established. The client will trust this public key certificate only if it is signed by a Certificate Authority trusted by the client. This Certificate Authority can either be a well-known CA or an organization's own internal CA.

SSL is designed to protect against "man in the middle" attacks. Network traffic between a client and server must not be modified in transit. But WAN Optimization by definition is a "man in the middle" as it modifies traffic it is optimizing. In order to optimize SSL traffic, the SteelHead appliances need to decrypt, optimize and re-encrypt the traffic over the WAN. Hence, the original SSL certificate from the SaaS server cannot be used to setup a session where the traffic is optimized.

So how to both optimize and secure SaaS traffic over the Internet? The solution is to replace the original SSL Certificate with a Proxy Certificate. This Proxy Certificate is presented by the Cloud (Akamai) that hosts the server side SteelHead. These Proxy Certificates are generated in the Cloud and can be signed either by the Cloud service (in this case by Akamai Technologies) or by an organization's own internal Certificate Authority. The client browsers of course will need to trust whichever CA is used by having its certificate already installed. Individual Proxy Certificates need to be generated for each unique SaaS provider as well as for different destination Hostnames. It is from the Riverbed Cloud Portal where Proxy Certificates can be generated.

SaaS Platform Proxy Certificates

This table allows you to generate Proxy Certificates for specific SaaS Hostnames. These Proxy Certificates will be signed by your dedicated Cloud-Hosted Certificate Authority.

Filter: [   ]   Clear

<< first < prev **1** next > last >>

Hostname	Proxy Certificate Status	Expires	
*.sharepoint.com	Active	Mar 27 21:00:15 2020 GMT	[Request New Proxy Certificate]
*.mail.microsoftonline.com	Active	Feb 11 02:24:36 2019 GMT	[Request New Proxy Certificate]
outlook.office.com	Active	Feb 11 02:24:37 2019 GMT	[Request New Proxy Certificate]
outlook.com	Active	Mar 27 21:00:14 2020 GMT	[Request New Proxy Certificate]
*.mail.emea.microsoftonline.com	---		[Request New Proxy Certificate]
mail.protection.outlook.com	---		[Request New Proxy Certificate]
*.sharepointonline.com	Active	Nov 13 16:19:05 2019 GMT	[Request New Proxy Certificate]
outlook.office365.com	Active	Feb 11 02:25:04 2019 GMT	[Request New Proxy Certificate]
*.outlook.com	Active	Feb 11 02:25:27 2019 GMT	[Request New Proxy Certificate]
*.mail.apac.microsoftonline.com	---		[Request New Proxy Certificate]

Figure 3-3 *SaaS Platform Proxy Certificates in Cloud Portal*

38

SteelHead SaaS Deployment Scenarios

Direct to Internet

SaaS application traffic originating from a branch office can either travel directly to the Internet or first be backhauled back to a data center. In the Direct to Internet scenario, a registered SteelHead appliance in the branch office intercepts the SaaS traffic on its LAN side and directly forwards the traffic to the Akamai cloud encapsulated in UDP over port 9545. Traffic in this case is NOT backhauled to the data center.

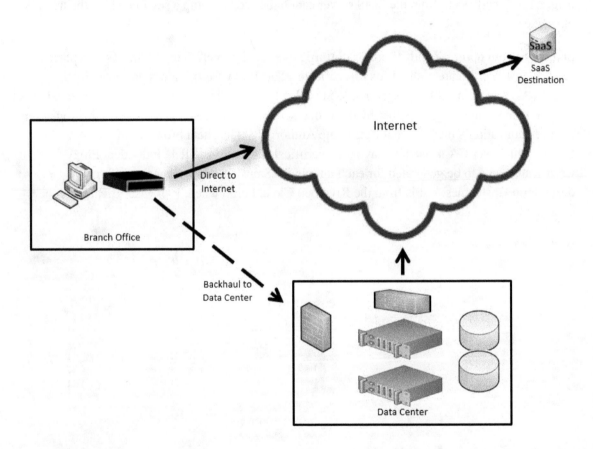

Figure 3-4 *Direct to Internet vs Backhaul*

Backhauling Traffic

Sometimes organizations require that all traffic going out to the Internet first be backhauled to a central data center where it can pass through a common firewall and security infrastructure. In this scenario, the SteelHead appliance in the branch office must NOT encapsulate SaaS traffic in UDP and forward it to the Akamai cloud. To handle this backhaul scenario, there is a setting on the SteelHead appliance called "Enable Cloud Acceleration Redirection" that needs to be checked OFF.

Figure 3-5 *Cloud Accelerator Control*

When "**Enable Cloud Acceleration Redirection**" is checked ON, a SteelHead appliance registered for SaaS optimization will redirect SaaS traffic to the Akamai cloud encapsulated in UDP over port 9545. Therefore, it should be checked ON when sending traffic directly to the Internet. When checked OFF, the SteelHead appliance will pass the traffic through unaltered. Therefore, it should be checked OFF when backhauling traffic back to the datacenter.

When optimizing SaaS traffic that is backhauled to the datacenter, there also needs to be a SteelHead appliance in the datacenter that has "**Enable Cloud Acceleration Redirection**" checked ON so it can forward SaaS application packets to the Akamai cloud over UDP port 9545.

Compatibility with Web Proxy Servers

Many enterprises today deploy web proxy servers to secure outgoing web traffic. Web proxy servers are typically deployed out of path and require either an explicit or transparent method to redirect web traffic to the proxy.

A transparent method of redirection will typically preserve the destination IP address of the packets and use GRE or another Layer 2 mechanism to send traffic to the web proxy. As long as the destination IP of the SaaS destination is preserved, SteelHead SaaS optimization can still function properly.

However, if using an explicit redirection mechanism that explicitly rewrites the destination IP to the IP of the Web Proxy before it is intercepted by a client side SteelHead, the SteelHead will no longer be able to identify SaaS traffic by inspecting the destination IP. PAC files are commonly used to redirect traffic to a web proxy from a web browser. If using a PAC file in a SteelHead SaaS environment, it is recommended to simply exclude SaaS URLs and domains from the list of destinations to be redirected to the proxy. The important point to remember is that the SteelHead needs to see the actual SaaS destination IP address in order to optimize SaaS traffic.

SteelHead Cloud Edition

Overview

When Amazon Web Services was first introduced in March 2006, it ushered in a new era for wide area networks. In this new era, WANs now needed to connect branch offices to both public and private data centers. The public data centers are of course owned and maintained by public cloud providers and can be located in regions around the world. In addition, cloud computing operates on an "operational expense" model versus a "capital expense" model where customers are charged on a per usage basis. Sometimes these charges are based on the amount of network traffic flowing to and from the cloud.

With that, WAN Optimization continues to play an important role in the era of cloud computing. Latency to cloud data centers can be just as great if not greater than to private data centers. And when charges are incurred based on traffic volumes flowing to and from the cloud, bandwidth optimization becomes even more crucial for minimizing operational costs.

SteelHead Cloud Edition (aka SteelHead–c) is a virtual instance of the SteelHead appliance that runs inside a cloud provider's infrastructure. Specifically, SteelHead Cloud can run either as an EC2 Instance inside Amazon Web Services (AWS) or as a Virtual Machine (VM) inside Microsoft Azure. SteelHead Cloud can peer with a client side SteelHead appliance running in a branch office location to deliver WAN Optimization for applications running inside the cloud.

Discovery Agent

A SteelHead-c instance running in AWS or Azure cannot be deployed physically in-path like a physical SteelHead appliance in a data center. So how does a SteelHead-c peer intercept and optimize connections coming from a client SteelHead? The answer is that it uses a Discovery Agent.

The Discovery Agent is software that is installed on a Windows or Linux server instance running in the cloud. Here's how it works:

1. When a client initiates a connection to an EC2 or VM server instance that has the Discovery Agent installed, the Discovery Agent will intercept the TCP SYN packet and check to see if it is marked with the Auto Discovery probe (0x4c) in the options field.
2. If so, the Discovery Agent will redirect the connection to a SteelHead-c running in AWS
3. SteelHead-c will then send a reply to the client side SteelHead with the IP address of SteelHead-c. The client side SteelHead will then peer with the SteelHead-c.
4. SteelHead-c then functions as a server side SteelHead optimizing application traffic to the server.

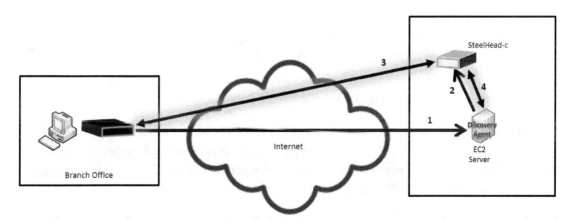

Figure 3-6 *SteelHead Cloud Discovery Agent*

Cloud Portal

But how does the Discovery Agent know which SteelHead-c to redirect the traffic to in the first place? The answer is that the Discovery Agent running on a cloud server gets SteelHead Cloud info from the Riverbed Cloud Portal.

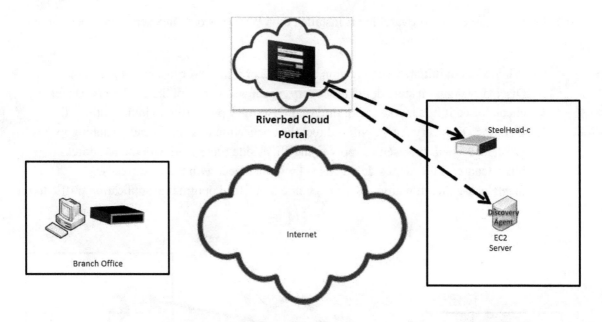

Figure 3-7 *Riverbed Cloud Portal*

Every SteelHead Cloud customer has access to a Riverbed Cloud Portal account. The Cloud Portal can be accessed at https://cloudportal.riverbed.com. It is from the Riverbed Cloud Portal where SteelHead Cloud customers can enter their AWS account info and provision SteelHead Cloud instances into their AWS account.

The Riverbed Cloud Portal is also used to create Optimization Groups. An Optimization Group specifies the list of Windows or Linux servers running in AWS EC2

Figure 3-8 *SteelHead Cloud Optimization Group*

Each Optimization Group also has a Client ID and Client Key. The Client ID and Client Key, along with the Cloud Portal Hostname or IP all need to be configured on the Discovery Agent. Once configured with these credentials, the Discover Agent will be able to communicate with the Cloud Portal and obtain the correct SteelHead-Cloud IPs for an AWS account.

SteelHead for SteelConnect

SteelConnect is Riverbed's SDWAN solution for connecting public and private cloud networks. SteelHead for SteelConnect delivers WAN Optimization for public cloud networks that are connected via SteelConnect. The two cloud networks supported by SteelHead for SteelConnect are AWS Virtual Private Cloud (VPC) and Azure Virtual Networks (VNet).

Like SteelHead Cloud, SteelHead for SteelConnect is deployed as a virtual instance inside the public cloud. It delivers WAN Optimization for applications running inside an AWS VPC or Azure Virtual Network. But with its tight integration with SteelConnect, the deployment of SteelHead for SteelConnect is much simpler. There is no need to install any Discovery Agents or setup Optimization Groups in the Riverbed Cloud Portal. Instead, SteelHead for SteelConnect is deployed along with a SteelConnect Gateway from the SteelConnect Manager. SteelConnect Manager is SteelConnect's easy to use management console that can be accessed from any standard web browser.

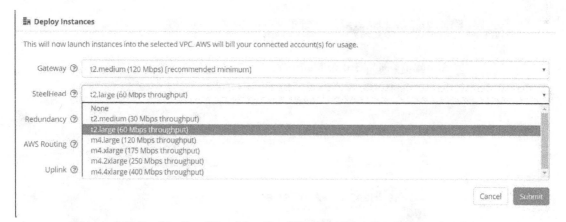

Figure 3-9 *Deploy SteelHead for SteelConnect from SteelConnect Manager*

Once deployed, the SteelConnect Gateway in the Cloud can automatically direct optimized traffic to the SteelHead for SteelConnect running inside a VPC or VNet. A SteelHead for SteelConnect can peer with a physical SteelHead running in a branch office or data center. It can also peer with another SteelHead for SteelConnect running in another VPC or VNet. This is all done automatically. There is no need to manually configure any route tables.

Virtual SteelHead appliance

Sometimes it is logistically difficult to ship a physical SteelHead appliance to a remote office located in another country with burdensome local tax or import processes. It may also be necessary to send a WAN optimization device into a ruggedized environment such as a military environment. This is where Virtual SteelHead appliance comes in. Virtual SteelHead appliance allows you to run RiOS on top of VMware ESX hypervisor or Microsoft Hyper-V on different hardware platforms. Since Virtual SteelHead appliance is purely software it can be a convenient way to quickly "ship" an appliance to very remote locations without the hassle of shipping and local import/export regulations.

SteelHead Mobile

SteelHead Mobile allows mobile laptop workers to experience the same LAN like performance when they are connected across the WAN through a VPN. SteelHead Mobile is essentially RiOS adapted for a Windows or Mac laptop. This mobile version of RiOS software installs and runs on the client machine. When the user connects back to the data center over a VPN, the mobile client will connect with the SteelHead appliance to perform optimization. The mobile client runs transparently in the background so end users for the most part do not have to do anything to configure the optimization.

SteelHead appliance Mobile requires the deployment of a SteelHead Mobile Controller in the data center. The Mobile Controller is responsible for creating the Mobile client software package. The configuration of the Mobile client is done through the Mobile Controller. In addition, the Mobile Controller also handles licensing and reporting for the Mobile clients plus a platform for managing the clients, relieving administrator from having to manage the end devices directly. But again, all optimization is performed strictly between the Mobile client and the SteelHead appliance.

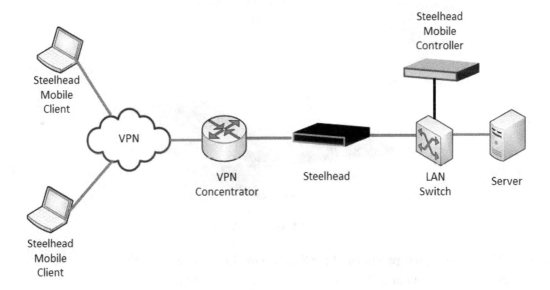

Figure 3-10 *SteelHead Mobile*

SteelFusion Edge

SteelFusion Edge is Riverbed's platform for Edge Computing. It combines compute, storage and WAN Optimization on a single hardware appliance deployed at an edge location. An edge location can be a branch office, construction site, ship at sea, mining site or any other location where work gets done.

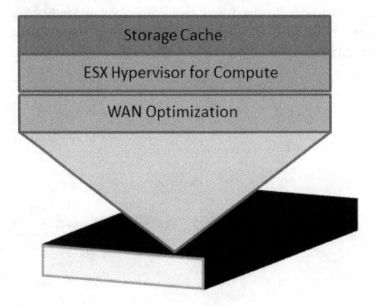

Figure 3-11 *SteelFusion Edge*

The WAN Optimization capabilities of the SteelFusion Edge are exactly the same as the SteelHead appliance. But in addition to optimizing application traffic over the WAN, SteelFusion Edge also hosts a VMware ESX based virtualization platform for running third party servers and services. SteelFusion Edge can also intelligently cache block level storage delivered from a remote data center. Together, the WAN Optimization, virtualization platform and intelligent storage caching offer a "one box solution" for edge locations that demand higher performance from local compute and storage.

Summary

Since its introduction in 2004, the SteelHead appliance has been adapted the meet the needs of new requirements brought on by Hybrid WANs connecting public and private clouds. The SteelHead CX appliance remains the leading WAN optimization product in the market today for optimizing connections between branch offices and private data centers.

SteelHead SaaS delivers optimization of popular SaaS applications such as Office 365.

SteelHead Cloud can deliver optimization from the branch office to applications running in AWS or Azure.

SteelHead for SteelConnect does the same for applications running in both AWS and Azure but with a much simpler deployment model.

SteelHead Mobile continues to provide WAN Optimization for mobile laptop users who remotely connect to applications running the data center over a VPN.

Virtual SteelHead appliances can run on VMware ESX or Microsoft Hyper-V hosts.

WAN Optimization can also be combined with a storage and compute platform via SteelFusion Edge.

In short, the Riverbed SteelHead product line offers the most comprehensive array of options for delivering WAN Optimization in any IT environment.

48

Chapter 4: SteelHead Deployment Options

In this chapter we discuss the different options for deploying a SteelHead appliance. But first we describe the network interfaces on the SteelHead appliance. We then describe the different SteelHead appliance deployment options: physically in-path, out of path and virtual in-path.

SteelHead appliance Network Interfaces

Every SteelHead appliance comes with a minimum of four GigE copper network interfaces. These interfaces are called the Primary, LAN, WAN and Auxiliary interfaces. Additional LAN and WAN interfaces (with several fiber options) are available on most models through add-in card(s).

Primary Interface

The Primary Interface is primarily used to provide out of band access to the SteelHead appliance management console. The Primary Interface is normally connected to a LAN switch via copper Ethernet cable and provides access to the SteelHead appliance Management Console GUI via HTTP or HTTPS. The Primary interface also provides access to the SteelHead appliance Command Line Interface (CLI) via SSH.

The Primary Interface also handles communication for other important SteelHead appliance features such as CIFS Pre-Population, Data Store Synchronization and Windows Domain Join.

In addition, the Primary Interface can also be used for optimizing TCP connections when the SteelHead appliance is deployed in server-side out of path mode which we describe shortly.

In-Path Interface (LAN/WAN)

The In-Path Interface is a logical network interface that is assigned to both the physical LAN and WAN interfaces on the SteelHead appliance. The LAN interface is typically connected to an internal LAN switch and the WAN interface to an outgoing WAN router. Inbound and outbound traffic typically flows in through one interface and the out the other.

A special IP address, called the In-Path IP address, is assigned to the In-Path interface. Both the LAN and WAN physical interfaces share this same In-Path IP address. The In-Path Interface is used for optimization and communication between the SteelHead appliances over the WAN.

50

The first LAN and WAN interfaces are named `lan0_0` and `wan0_0`. The interfaces on the second pair are name `lan0_1` and `wan0_1`. If an additional 4 port network interface card is added the interfaces on the next pair are named `lan1_0` and `wan1_0` and so on.

All SteelHead hardware appliances use fail to wire NIC cards for the LAN/WAN interfaces. Fail to wire NIC cards ensure that traffic will continue to flow through the SteelHead appliance in the event that RiOS or the entire appliance shuts down. In addition, the NIC cards can be configure to *not* fail to wire. This is also known as fail to block. Fail to block can be useful for redirecting traffic in networks with redundant design.

Auxiliary Interface

The Auxiliary Interface can be considered as a backup interface or an interface to a dedicated management network compared to the Primary interface. It is not commonly used. But if used, the Auxiliary Interface needs to be assigned an IP address with a different subnet from the Primary interface.

Deployment Options

We now describe the different deployment options for the SteelHead appliance.

Physical In-Path

Most SteelHead appliances are deployed physically in-path or "inline" between a switch and a router.

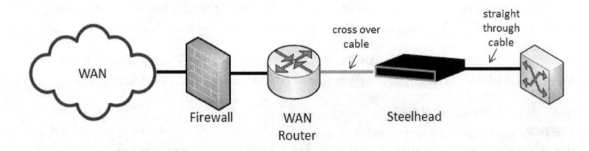

Figure 4-1 *Physical In-Path SteelHead appliance*

This option is the simplest to deploy. In a physical in-path deployment the SteelHead appliance is physically inline between the LAN switch and the outgoing WAN router. A straight through cable connects the SteelHead appliance LAN side interface to the LAN switch. A crossover cable connects the SteelHead appliance's WAN side interface to the WAN router. The SteelHead appliance must be deployed behind the firewall or any other device that encrypts the traffic over the WAN. By being in-path, the SteelHead appliance "sees" all traffic going in and out of the local network before it goes out to the WAN.

Advantage

The biggest advantage in choosing a physical in-path deployment is that it is the simplest and easiest option to deploy. No configuration changes need to be made on neighboring routers or switches. The deployment is completely transparent to other devices.

Disadvantage

Deploying a SteelHead appliance physically in-path requires a brief interruption in WAN connectivity as the SteelHead appliance is inserted between the switch and the router. And while all SteelHead appliances come equipped with fail to wire bypass NIC cards, a SteelHead appliance deployed physically in-path can still be considered a potential single point of failure.

Server Side Out of Path (SSOP)

A server side SteelHead appliance can also be deployed physically out of path. This is called a Server-side Out of Path (SSOP) deployment. All SteelHead CX, Virtual SteelHead and SteelHead Cloud appliances support SSOP. In an out of path deployment, the SteelHead appliance's Primary Interface is connected directly to a LAN switch. There are no additional connections to the router or firewall.

Because it is deployed out of path, the SteelHead appliance cannot automatically intercept and optimize traffic from client side SteelHead appliances. Client side SteelHead appliances need to have a Fixed-target rule configured to optimize traffic with a server-side SteelHead appliance that is deployed out of path. This fixed-target rule is directed towards the server side SteelHead appliance's Primary IP address listening on port 7810. The steps for setting up fixed-target rules are described in chapter 5.

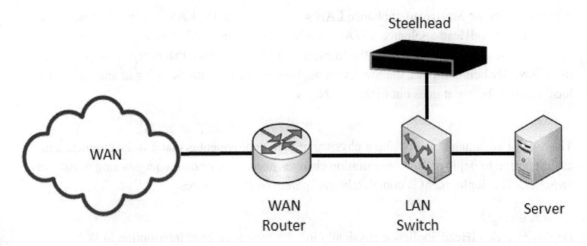

Figure 4-2 *Server Side Out of Path SteelHead appliance*

In a SSOP deployment, the SteelHead appliance will establish an outer TCP session with the server just as in an in-path deployment. However, a key difference in an SSOP deployment is that the SteelHead appliance will perform a Network Address Translation of the original client IP address to the SteelHead appliance's Primary IP address. In other words, the original client IP address is not visible to the server. The server sees the SteelHead appliance's Primary IP address as the source instead.

Advantage

The primary advantage of choosing the server side out of path option is that it does not require any interruption to network traffic to install. Unlike the in-path option, the out of path option only requires a single connection to an open port on the existing LAN switch. There is no need to break the connection between a switch and a router to insert the SteelHead appliance in between. No existing cables need to be unplugged to deploy a SteelHead appliance out of path.

Disadvantage

The main drawback of using a server side out of path deployment is that it will only work for server side SteelHead appliances. A client side SteelHead appliance cannot be deployed physically out of path unless there is a way to redirect client side traffic to the SteelHead appliance which we will discuss later. For this reason, the out of path deployment option is more commonly referred to as the Server Side out of Path (SSOP) option.

In addition, a fixed-target rule must be configured on each client side SteelHead appliance optimizing with a server side SteelHead appliance that is deployed out of path. This makes SSOP deployments less scalable if client side SteelHead appliances need to be deployed at multiple remote sites.

Hybrid Mode

A SteelHead appliance can also simultaneously function as an in-path and as a server-side out of path SteelHead appliance. This is known as Hybrid mode. When in Hybrid mode, a SteelHead appliance can both intercept TCP connections on the client side and respond to Auto Discovery probes on the server side just like an in path SteelHead appliance. A SteelHead appliance in hybrid mode will also respond to fixed-target rules on its Primary interface just like a server side out of path SteelHead appliance.

Why use Hybrid Mode? Sometimes a SteelHead appliance needs to be deployed in-path on the client side in order to intercept TCP connections to be optimized coming from local client hosts. However, this same SteelHead appliance may not be in the direct path or in line with servers located in a DMZ that require optimized connections with clients on the other side of the WAN. In cases such as this, the SteelHead appliance can be deployed in Hybrid mode to optimize both types of connections.

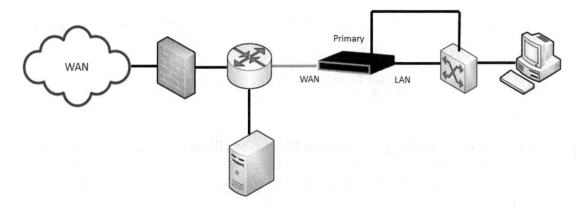

Figure 4-3 *Hybrid Mode*

Virtual In-Path

SteelHead appliances can also be deployed virtually in-path. In a virtual in-path deployment the SteelHead appliance is deployed physically out of path. It has a single connection to a router or switch. The SteelHead appliance is not inline and no interruption to network traffic is required to deploy the SteelHead appliance. To direct traffic to the SteelHead appliance, a re-direction mechanism is used on the router.

This re-direction mechanism can either be WCCP or policy based routing (PBR). WCCP is a protocol developed by Cisco® for using a router to redirect traffic to another device on the network (in this case the SteelHead appliance). Policy based routing (PBR) involves configuring special routing rules on the router to redirect traffic to the SteelHead appliance.

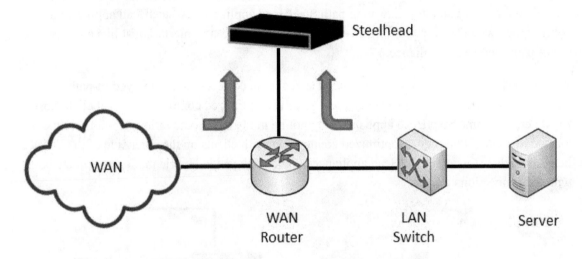

Figure 4-4 *Virtual In-Path SteelHead appliance*

The reason it's called virtual in-path is because from the SteelHead appliance's perspective the SteelHead appliances seem inline and can automatically intercept traffic. No special rules (such as Fixed-target rules) are needed on the SteelHead appliances to direct traffic to a peer SteelHead appliance.

Advantage

The main advantage of using virtual in-path is that no interruption in network traffic is required to deploy the SteelHead appliance. Only a single connection is needed between the SteelHead appliance and the switch or router. The SteelHead appliance does not present any possibility of being a potential single point of failure. And unlike Server Side Out-of-Path deployments, Virtual In-Path deployments will work for both client and server side SteelHead appliances.

Disadvantage

Virtual in-path deployments are more complex to deploy. They require the network administrator to configure either WCCP or PBR on their router. Depending on the traffic volume, virtual in-path deployments can also put additional CPU load on either the router or SteelHead appliance. For this reason, the virtual in-path mode is considered to be an advanced deployment option of the SteelHead appliance.

Load Balancing and High Availability

There are other advanced deployment options that can be used to provide load balancing and high availability for the SteelHead appliances. For example, multiple SteelHead appliances can be deployed in the data center for load balancing. These multiple SteelHead appliances are all deployed out of path. In front of these SteelHeads is a special appliance that is deployed in path called the Riverbed® Interceptor® appliance. The Interceptor appliance specializes in performing load balancing across multiple SteelHeads.

A pair of SteelHead appliances can also be deployed as a serial cluster for high availability. In a serial cluster two SteelHeads are deployed in path with one in front of the other. Their data stores can also be synchronized so that one SteelHead can take over for the other in the event that one of them fails.

Summary

All SteelHead appliances come with a Primary, Auxiliary and at least one pair of LAN/WAN network interfaces. SteelHead appliances can be deployed physically in path, out of path or virtually in-path. A SteelHead appliance can also be deployed in hybrid mode. The physical in-path deployment option is the most common deployment option as it is the simplest to deploy. There are also options for deploying the SteelHeads for load balancing and high availability.

Chapter 5: Deploying the SteelHead appliance

This chapter gives step by step instructions for deploying the SteelHead appliance. It starts with the initial task of sizing an appropriate SteelHead appliance model. It then describes steps for achieving the most common task – installing a SteelHead appliance in-path – and moves to some more advanced tasks such as setting up optimization for encrypted environments as well as for SteelHead SaaS. This section assumes that SteelHead appliance concepts are understood and it focuses on helping the IT professional (who may be new to WAN optimization) get a successful SteelHead appliance deployment up and running.

SteelHead Appliance Installation & Setup

This section gives instructions for selecting, installing and setting up a SteelHead appliance.

How to Size a SteelHead appliance

Overview

Before installing a SteelHead appliance you must first select the appropriately sized SteelHead appliance model. Regardless of model, all SteelHead appliances run a version of the RiOS software. When choosing the right SteelHead appliance, the most important differences between each model to consider are:

- Optimized TCP Connection Count Capacity
- Optimized WAN Capacity
- Data Store Capacity

TCP Connections

Each SteelHead appliance can optimized up to a limited number of TCP connections. A good way to estimate the number of connections needed at a location is to count the number of users. A typical branch office user probably needs to connect to an email server, a few file servers and an application server. A rule of thumb is 7-10 TCP connections per user. You can get a more precise estimate through Netflow-based tools like Riverbed Cascade Profiler.

If the number of TCP connections going through a SteelHead appliance exceeds the limit, the additional connections will pass through the SteelHead appliance un-optimized. The SteelHead appliance does not drop or block traffic.

Optimized WAN Capacity

The optimized WAN capacity of a SteelHead appliance model refers to optimized traffic only. In other words traffic that has been de-duplicated and/or compressed. It does not include un-optimized or pass-through traffic. Therefore, it is quite common to deploy a SteelHead appliance on a link where the available bandwidth is slightly greater than the optimized WAN capacity of the SteelHead appliance.

However there are times where the data is not very compressible or where a lot of bandwidth is available and the goal is to maximize throughput such as in backup and recovery. In situations such as these it is recommended that the SteelHead appliance's WAN capacity matches the available bandwidth in order to maximize bandwidth utilization and throughput.

Data Store Capacity

Each SteelHead appliance has reserved persistent storage for the data store. The data store stores the dictionary of data segments used by SDR. Since the data store stores only unique data blocks the size of the data store can be much smaller than the total volume of data passing through the WAN. As a general rule, the data store should be roughly 1/5 the size of the total data set. For example, if SteelHead appliances are used optimize file access to a file server containing 200GB of files then a data store of at least 40GB is recommended.

Sizing for the Branch Office

When sizing a SteelHead appliance for the branch office, the number of optimized TCP connections is usually the most important parameter. This is because additional users who exceed the TCP connection count capacity will get un-optimized (and slow) traffic.

Sizing for the Data Center

SteelHead appliances are usually deployed in a hub and spoke network with one larger SteelHead appliance at the data center optimizing with multiple smaller branch SteelHead appliances. SteelHead appliances at the data center are typically sized to according to the aggregate amount of TCP connections coming in from the different branch offices.

Sizing for Backup and Replication (DR)

When sizing for a backup and replication scenario, the WAN capacity and data store size become much more important than the TCP connection count. Backup and replication solutions typically use just a few connections to push through much larger amounts of traffic. But in addition to connection count, data size and WAN capacity, there are many other important parameters that need to be taken into account before selecting the right SteelHead appliance for DR. These factors include expected LAN side throughput, backup/replication solution used, total dataset size, and so on. For this reason, Riverbed usually recommends filling out a standard DR questionnaire to gather all the necessary info before selecting the appropriate SteelHead appliance. At high bandwidths you will definitely want to consult with an expert for cluster design and implementation.

How to Install a SteelHead appliance Physically In-Path

Overview

SteelHead appliances are most commonly deployed in-path between the local LAN switch and WAN router. It is the simplest and easiest deployment option.

The appliances are shipped with a grey null modem cable. This cable can be used to the SteelHead appliance's console serial port to launch the configuration wizard.

The SteelHead appliances do not come shipped with static IP addresses. However, the Primary interface by default does have DHCP enabled.

Configure Appliance

1. Plug in appliance to power supply.
2. Connect the serial cable to the console port on the SteelHead appliance and to your desktop or laptop.
3. If using a terminal emulator on your laptop you should be able to launch the SteelHead appliance console using following terminal settings:

```
9600 bps
8 data bits
Parity none
Stop bits 1
vt100 emulation
No flow control
```

4. Login as `admin/password`

5. If asked "`Do you want to auto-configure using CMC?`" Enter no.
6. If asked "`Do you want to use the configuration wizard for initial configuration?`" Enter yes. Go to step 8.
7. If you see a prompt instead, run the configuration wizard via CLI

```
>enable
#configure terminal
(config) # configuration jump-start
```

8. The configuration wizard should look like this:

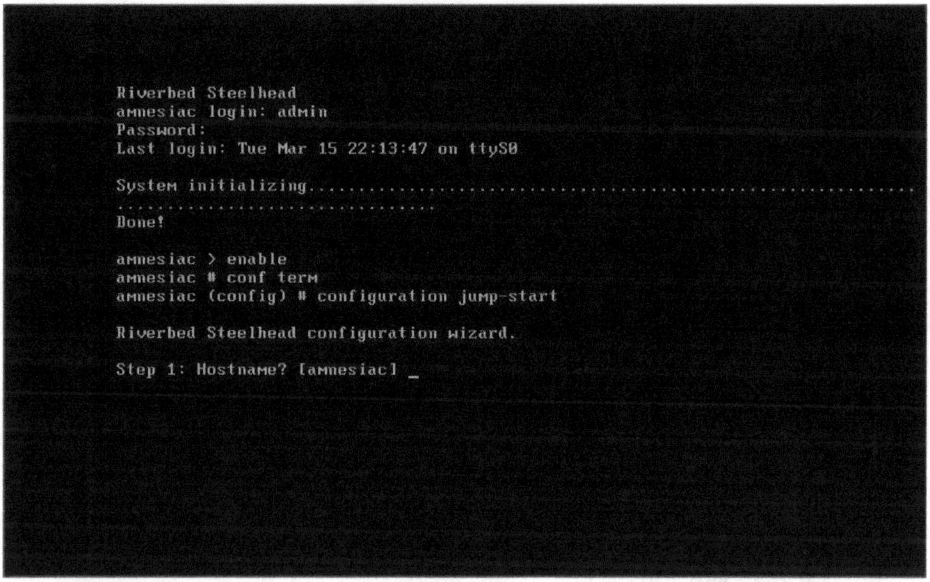

Figure 5-1 *Riverbed SteelHead appliance Configuration Wizard*

9. Enter **Hostname**.
10. Recommend **no** for DHCP.
11. Enter **Primary IP Address**. The Primary IP Address is used to access the management console.
12. Enter Netmask for Primary IP Address.
13. Enter default gateway for Primary IP Address.
14. Enter Primary DNS server (optional)
15. Enter domain name. (optional)
16. Changing admin password is recommended.
17. SMTP is optional.
18. Notification email is optional.
19. Set primary interface speed to auto.
20. Set primary duplex to auto.
21. Enter '**yes**' to activate in-path configuration.
22. Set **in-path IP address**. The in-path address is a logical interface assigned to the LAN/WAN interfaces.
23. Enter In-Path Netmask.
24. Enter In-Path Default Gateway.
25. Set in-path LAN interface speed and duplex to auto (especially with gigabit Ethernet). Otherwise, the recommended in-path speed is **100** and **full** to match the other side.

26. Hit <enter> to save changes and exit.

Install Into Network

1. Plug straight-through cable to connect switch to SteelHead appliance Primary port.
2. Plug straight-through cable to connect switch to SteelHead appliance LAN port.
3. Plug crossover cable from SteelHead appliance WAN port to router.

Verify Connectivity

1. Connect to SteelHead appliance CLI.
2. Ping server from client to server in-path and vice versa. For example:

```
#ping -I <client in-path IP address> <server in-path IP
address>
```

3. Ping client side SteelHead appliance from server side SteelHead appliance and vice versa.
4. Ping client side SteelHead appliance from client and vice versa.
5. Ping server side SteelHead appliance from server and vice versa.

Management Console

1. Open web browser.
2. Login to management console using `http://<primary ip address>` for the URL.
3. Click **Home**.
4. Verify Status is "**Healthy**."

How to Upgrade the SteelHead appliance

Overview

Riverbed regularly releases upgrades to the RiOS software. Software upgrades are recommended to address known issues and take advantage of new features.

RiOS is backwards compatible. For example, a SteelHead appliance running RiOS 7.0 will optimize traffic with a peer SteelHead appliance running RiOS 6.5. But in general, both SteelHead appliances should be running the same RiOS version in order to enable most updated features of a newer RiOS version.

Upgrading RiOS is simple.

Download New Software Version

1. Login to Riverbed Support site https://support.riverbed.com.

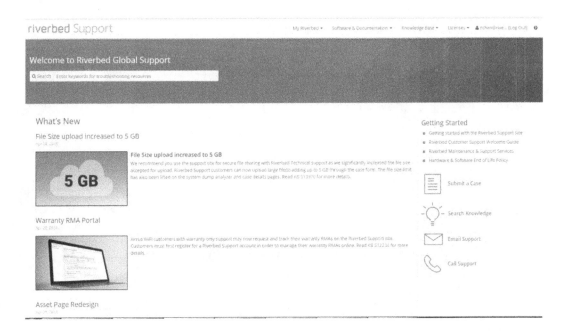

Figure 5-2 *Riverbed Support Site*

2. If you are new to the site you will need to click "registration" and register. To register, you will need your corporate email address and a serial number that is under support contract.

3. Click **Software & Documentation > SteelHead.** Then click **SteelHead CX/GX** on the left menu. Click Software tab and select a software version to download a SteelHead Appliance Software image.

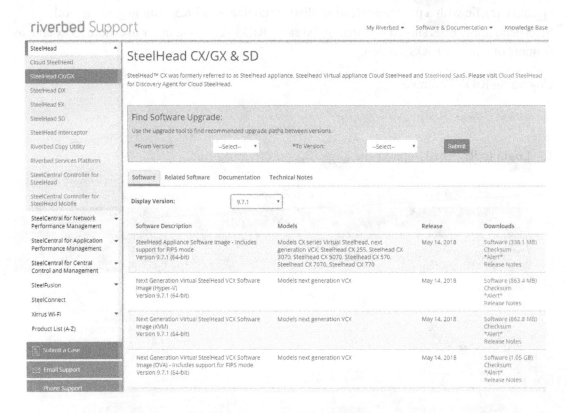

Figure 5-3 *Download Software from Riverbed Support Site*

Install Upgrade

1. Login to the SteelHead appliance and go to **Administration > Maintenance > Software Upgrade**.

2. Click "From URL" or "From Local File" to upload the upgrade image.

3. Click Install. After install is complete you will need to reboot the SteelHead appliance.

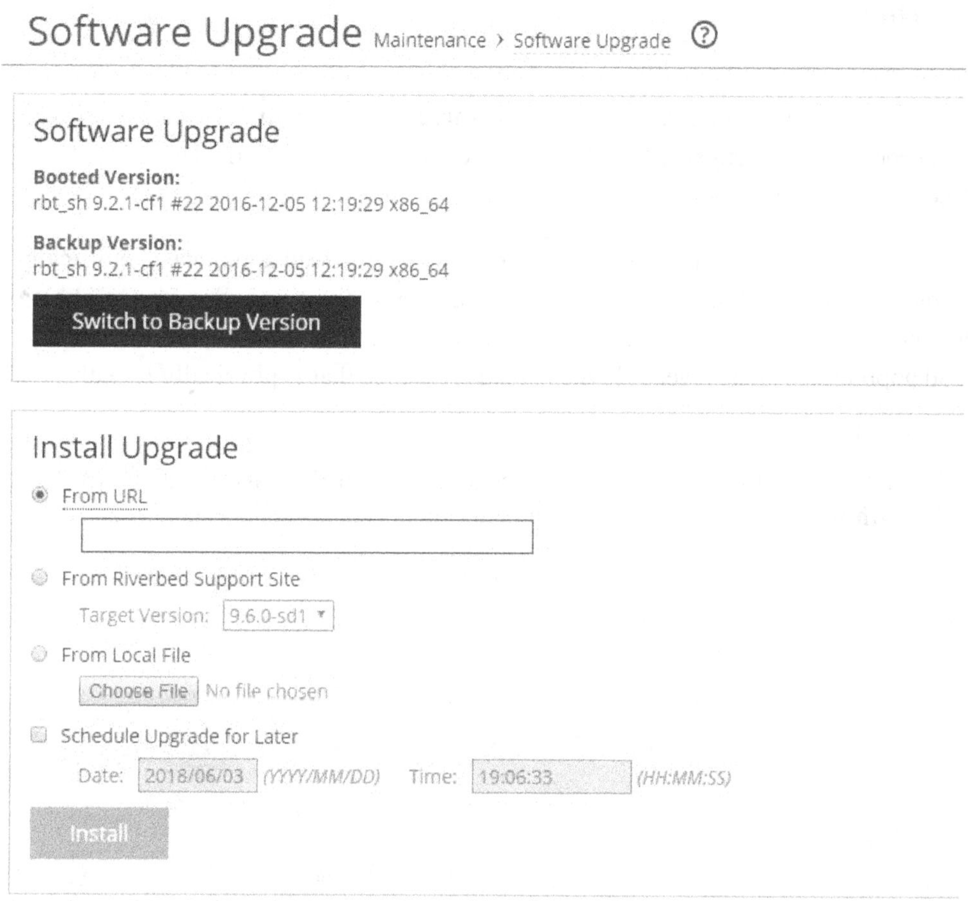

Software Upgrade Maintenance › Software Upgrade ⊙

Software Upgrade

Booted Version:
rbt_sh 9.2.1-cf1 #22 2016-12-05 12:19:29 x86_64

Backup Version:
rbt_sh 9.2.1-cf1 #22 2016-12-05 12:19:29 x86_64

Switch to Backup Version

Install Upgrade

⦿ From URL

[   ]

◯ From Riverbed Support Site

Target Version: [9.6.0-sd1 ▾]

◯ From Local File

[Choose File] No file chosen

☐ Schedule Upgrade for Later

Date: [2018/06/03] *(YYYY/MM/DD)* Time: [19:06:33] *(HH:MM:SS)*

[Install]

Figure 5-4 *Software Upgrade*

How to Setup a Fixed-Target Rule

Overview

Fixed-target rules are most commonly used in server side out of path deployments. Fixed-target rules are needed on the client side SteelHead appliance in order for it to peer with a server side SteelHead appliance that is not physically in-path.

Fixed-target rules can also be used when the server side SteelHead appliance is physically in-path. Sometimes a firewall may block the SteelHead appliance's auto discovery probe preventing automatic peering. When this happens a fixed-target rule can be used to peer a client side SteelHead appliance with a server side SteelHead appliance that is physically in-path.

Steps to Configure

1. Login to client side SteelHead appliance and go to **Optimization > Network Services > In-Path Rules**.

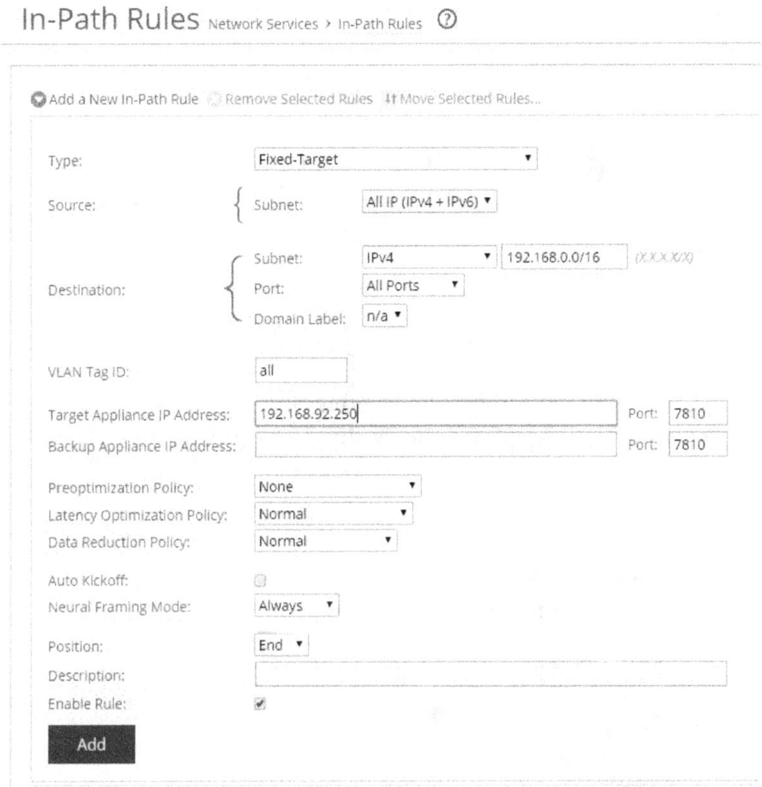

Figure 5-5 *In-Path Rules*

2. Click "Add a New In-Path rule" tab.
3. In the **Add New Rule** box, select type "Fixed-Target."
4. In the Target Appliance IP field enter the In-Path IP or Primary address of the server side SteelHead appliance. If using In-Path IP, enter port **7800** (for hybrid deployment). If using Primary IP, enter port **7810** (for SSOP deployment).
5. Specify Destination Subnet.
6. Click "Add Rule" button.
7. Check that your new fixed-target rule is above the default rule. If you have not added any other rules, the fixed-target rule should be #4 on the list.
8. Click the "Save" button on the bottom right. (No service restart required)

9. If using the Primary IP, go to **Optimization > Network Services > General Service Settings** on the server side appliance. Enable Out-of-Path support on server side appliance. Click "Apply."

Out-of-Path Settings

☑ Enable Out-of-Path Support *(server-side appliances only)*

Figure 5-6 *Enable Out-of-Path Support*

10. Restart service on server side SteelHead appliance.
11. The client side SteelHead appliance will now optimize TCP traffic with the target IP on the server side appliance.

Note that there are many more configuration settings in the in-path rules, should you need to customize which subnets are optimized, or other optimization parameters.

Optimizing Secure Traffic

How to Optimize Secure Windows Traffic (Signed SMB and Encrypted MAPI)

Overview

The two most common types of secure traffic in a Windows environment are SMB Signed traffic and Encrypted MAPI traffic.

SMB Signing

SMB Signing is a method used to secure SMB (CIFS) traffic. It is enabled by default on Windows domain controllers. It secures traffic by using cryptographic methods to digitally sign SMB packets to protect against man in the middle attacks. Since the SteelHead appliances intercept and proxy TCP connections between a client and a server, they can be considered a "man in the middle."

With SMB signing enabled, the SteelHead appliances can still perform data and transport streamlining. But they normally cannot perform application streamlining. Since SMB Signing is designed to ensure that packets reaching the CIFS server originated from the actual client, the SteelHead appliance cannot initiate its own requests to the server to perform transaction prediction. If SMB signing is in use you will often see a red triangle indicating a protocol error in the SteelHead appliance Current Connections report:

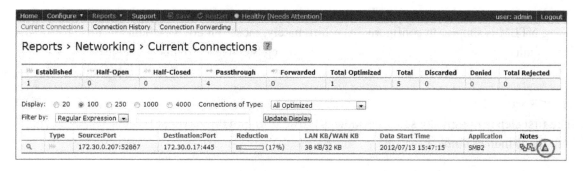

Figure 5-7 *Current Connections Report*

Encrypted MAPI

Exchange 2010 encrypts MAPI traffic by default. The SteelHead appliances cannot perform any data reduction or latency optimization on encrypted traffic. If Encrypted MAPI is in use, you should see a Reduction of 0% for MAPI connections in the Current Connections report.

The ability to optimize both SMB signed and Encrypted MAPI was first introduced in RiOS version 5.5. Since then Riverbed has continually added new features to make it easier to configure and to support the latest updates to Windows security. For this reason it is strongly recommended that you upgrade to at least RiOS version 7.0.3 or higher when optimizing secure Windows traffic. The following instructions assume that all SteelHead appliances are running RiOS 7.0.3 or higher.

Windows Authentication Methods: NTLM & Kerberos

There are two types of authentication methods used by Windows to secure traffic: NTLM and Kerberos. NTLM is the default authentication method used by Windows XP and Vista clients. Kerberos is the default authentication method used by Windows 7 clients. Kerberos is considered to be a more secure authentication protocol than NTLM. With the increased security comes additional complexity in optimizing traffic authenticated by Kerberos. Optimizing these connections requires the creation of a special Active Directory user that must be added to the server side SteelHead appliance. This special AD user must either have Delegation or Replication privileges.

Optimizing connections authenticated by NTLM on the other hand does *not* require the creation of a Delegate or Replication user. For this reason, optimizing secure connections authenticated using NTLM is simpler to configure. And fortunately, most Windows 7 clients that use Kerberos by default can also be negotiated by servers (including SteelHead appliances) to use NTLM instead.

Join Server Side SteelHead appliance into Domain

The first step in optimizing secure Windows traffic is to join the server side SteelHead appliance into the Windows domain.

1. On the server side SteelHead appliance go to **Configure > Networking > Windows Domain**.
2. Make sure Primary DNS IP address is correct.
3. Fill in fields for Domain Name, Login and Password.

4. Make sure clock on the SteelHead is within 30 seconds of the clock on the domain controller.
5. For the "Join Account Type" field it is recommended that you join the domain as an RODC or BDC in order to support NTLM Transparent Mode.

NTLM Transparent Mode

In NTLM Transparent mode, NTLM is the authentication method used end to end from the client to the server. NTLM is used between the client and server side SteelHead appliance as well as between the server side SteelHead appliance and server. By joining the SteelHead appliance as an RODC or BDC, the SteelHead appliance will be able to negotiate with both clients and servers from the same domain to use NTLM instead of Kerberos. NTLM Transparent mode will *not* work with Windows 7 clients unless the SteelHead appliance joins the domain as an RODC/BDC.

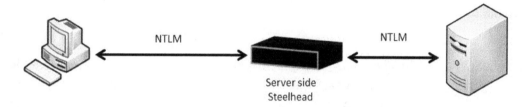

Figure 5-8 *NTLM Transparent Mode*

It is recommended to always enable NTLM Transparent mode (even in a Kerberos environment) in case the client and server fall back to using NTLM instead of Kerberos.

NTLM Delegation Mode

If you do not join the SteelHead appliance as an RODC/BDC and join it as a workstation instead, the SteelHead appliance can still authenticate the client using NTLM but it will not be able to negotiate with the server to use NTLM. If that is the case you will then have to configure a Delegate user for the SteelHead appliance so that it can still authenticate with the server using Kerberos on behalf of an original client user using NTLM. This is called NTLM Delegation mode.

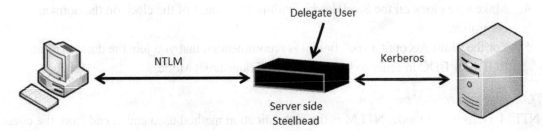

Figure 5-9 *NTLM Delegation Mode*

Prior to RiOS 7, NTLM Delegation mode was the only means to optimize secure Windows traffic using Kerberos. With RiOS 7, a replication user can be used instead.

A SteelHead appliance configured to use a replication user with NTLM Transparent mode enabled *does not* need a delegate user.

End to End Kerberos

Sometimes a Windows client can only use Kerberos and cannot be negotiated to use NTLM due to a group policy or because NTLM has been disabled. Kerberos must be used end to end from the client to the server. This is called end to end Kerberos. The Riverbed feature for optimizing end to end Kerberos environments is called "native Kerberos." In native Kerberos a special Active Directory user called a replication user needs to be created and added to the SteelHead appliance. We discuss the steps for configuring the replication user later.

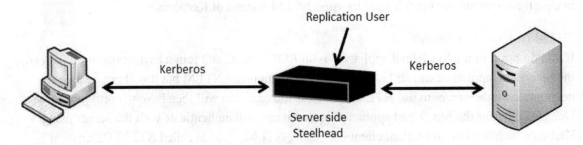

Figure 5-10 *End to End Kerberos*

Enable NTLM Transparent Mode

Assuming that the server side SteelHead appliance has joined the domain as an RODC/BDC and End to End Kerberos is NOT required, the SteelHead appliance can now negotiate with Windows clients and servers from the same domain to use NTLM. The next step is to configure SMB Signing and Encrypted MAPI to use NTLM Transparent Mode. Again, in NTLM Transparent mode, NTLM is the authentication mechanism used between the client and server side SteelHead appliance as well as between the server side SteelHead appliance and server.

SMB Signing

1. Go to **Configure > Optimization > SMB1/SMB2** on server side SteelHead appliance
2. Check "Enable SMB/ Signing"
3. Under SMB Signing check "NTLM Transparent Mode."

Encrypted MAPI

1. Go to **Configure > Optimization > MAPI** on *both* client side SteelHead appliance and server side SteelHead appliance.
2. Check "Enable Encrypted Optimization."
3. Check "NTLM Transparent Mode."

At this point you should now be able to fully optimize SMB Signed and Encrypted MAPI traffic without any protocol errors. If you do still see protocol errors in the Current Connections report, it is probably because end to end Kerberos is required and the SteelHead appliance was not able to negotiate with the Windows client and server to use NTLM Authentication. If this is the case you must now configure a replication user and add this user to the server side SteelHead appliance.

The replication user is used by the SteelHead appliance so that it can obtain the machine account credentials it needs to transparently participate in the key exchange between the client and the server. This allows the SteelHead appliance to optimize encrypted or signed Windows traffic while maintaining security.

Configure Replication User in Active Directory

Below are the steps for setting up a replication user in Active Directory.

Domain Controller

Create Replication User Account
1. Login to your Windows Domain Controller and launch Active Directory Users and Computers.
2. Under the domain and User folder create a user, i.e., "replication_user."

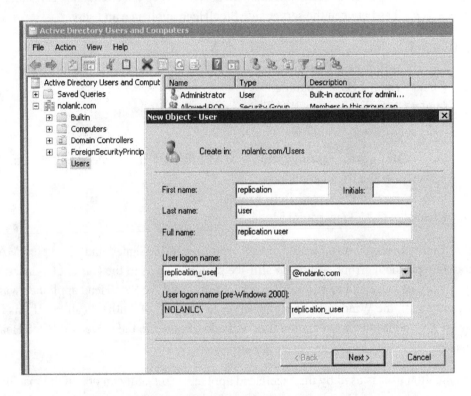

Figure 5-11 *Adding a replication user*

Delegation Control Wizard
1. Launch Active Directory Users and Computers and click domain name.
2. Right Click **Delegate Control...** to launch Delegation Control Wizard.

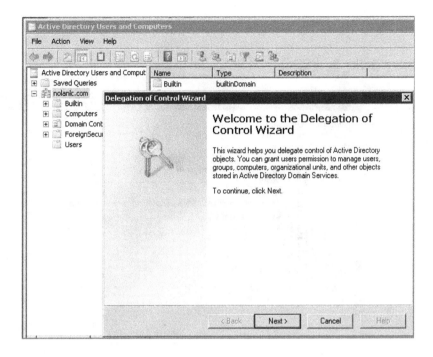

Figure 5-12 *Delegation Control Wizard*

3. Add replication user to Users and Groups.

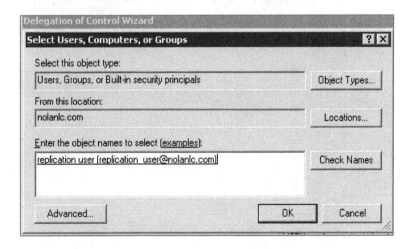

Figure 5-13 *Add replication user to Group*

4. Tasks to Delegate > Select "Create a custom task to delegate."

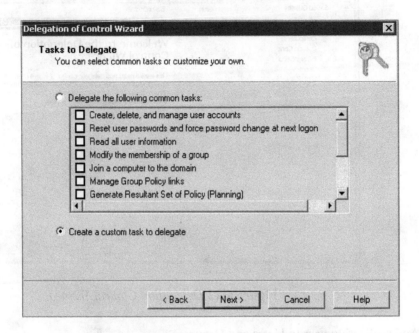

Figure 5-14 *Create a custom task to delegate*

5. Active Directory Object Type -> Select "This folder, existing objects…" and click "Next."

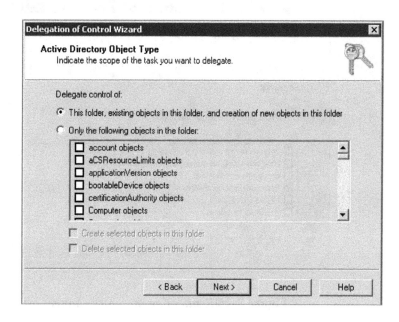

Figure 5-15 *Active Directory Object Type*

6. Permissions: Select **"General"** and scroll down Permissions to select **"Replicating Directory Changes"** and **"Replicating Directory Changes All."**

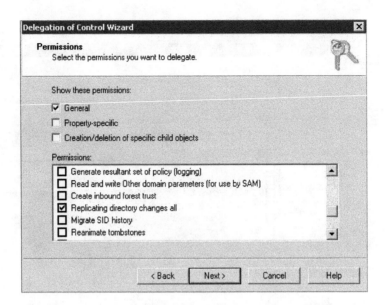

Figure 5-16 *Replicating directory changes all*

Enable Kerberos Authentication Support

SMB Signing
1. Go to **Optimization > Protocols > SMB2/3** on SSH
2. Under SMB Signing check "Enable Kerberos Authentication Support."

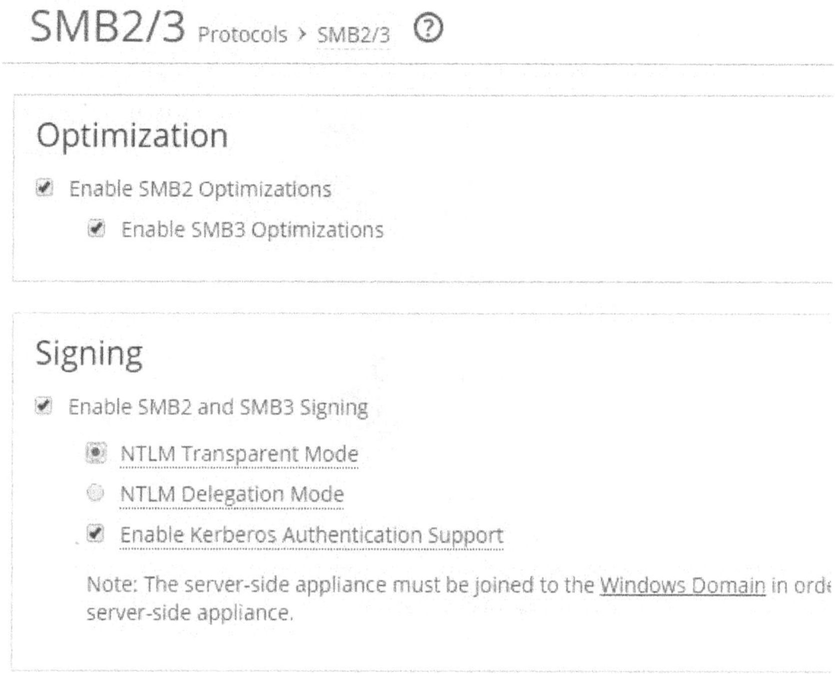

SMB2/3 Protocols > SMB2/3 ⓘ

Optimization

☑ Enable SMB2 Optimizations

☑ Enable SMB3 Optimizations

Signing

☑ Enable SMB2 and SMB3 Signing

◉ NTLM Transparent Mode

◯ NTLM Delegation Mode

☑ Enable Kerberos Authentication Support

Note: The server-side appliance must be joined to the Windows Domain in orde
server-side appliance.

Figure 5-17 *Enable Kerberos Authentication Support*

Encrypted MAPI

1. Go to **Optimization > Protocols > MAPI** on *both* the client and server side SteelHead appliances.

2. Check "Enable Kerberos Authentication Support."

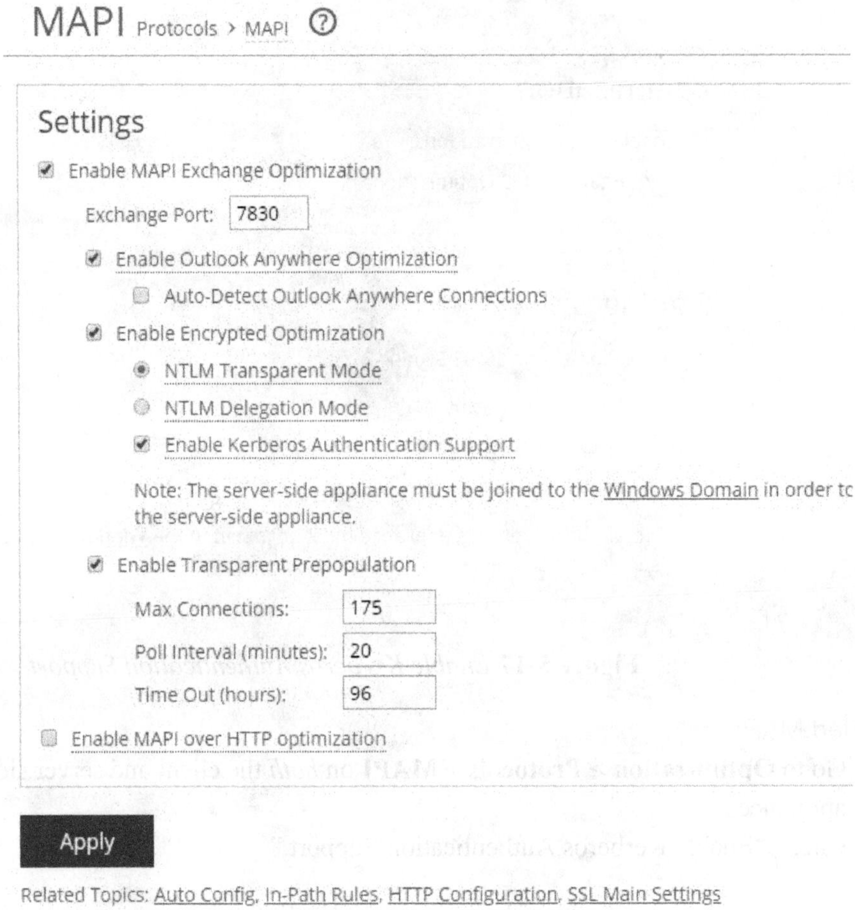

MAPI Protocols > MAPI ⑦

Settings

☑ Enable MAPI Exchange Optimization

    Exchange Port: `7830`

    ☑ Enable Outlook Anywhere Optimization

        ☐ Auto-Detect Outlook Anywhere Connections

    ☑ Enable Encrypted Optimization

        ◉ NTLM Transparent Mode

        ○ NTLM Delegation Mode

        ☑ Enable Kerberos Authentication Support

        Note: The server-side appliance must be joined to the Windows Domain in order to
        the server-side appliance.

    ☑ Enable Transparent Prepopulation

        Max Connections: `175`

        Poll Interval (minutes): `20`

        Time Out (hours): `96`

☐ Enable MAPI over HTTP optimization

[Apply]

Related Topics: Auto Config, In-Path Rules, HTTP Configuration, SSL Main Settings

Figure 5-18 *Enable Kerberos Authentication Support for MAPI*

Replication User Configuration

The next step is to add the replication user to the server side SteelHead appliance.

1. Go to **Optimization > Active Directory > Service Accounts** on the server side SteelHead.
2. In the Kerberos section click "Add a New User."

3. Active Directory domain name – i.e.,"*.test.companyname.com" or "test.companyname.com." This is the domain that replication user is allowed to replicate from.
4. User Domain – generally at root of active directory domain, i.e., "companyname.com." This is the domain the replication user belongs to.
5. If password changes in AD, password needs to be updated in SteelHead appliance too.
6. Check "Enable RODC Password Replication Policy Support" if password replication policy is in place.

You should now be able to fully optimize secure Windows traffic authenticated using End to End Kerberos with no protocol errors (red triangles).

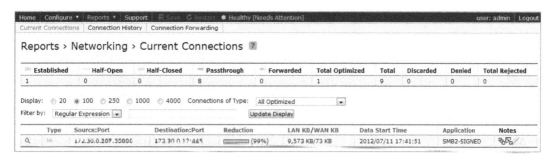

Figure 5-19 *No Protocol Errors*

Recommended Best Practices

- Always upgrade to RiOS 7.0.3 or higher to optimize secure Windows traffic.
- Always join server-side SteelHead appliance as an RODC or BDC whenever possible. That way you can use NTLM Transparent Mode and not have to worry about configuring a Replication or Delegate User to handle Kerberos authentication. (This is of course assuming that End to End Kerberos is not required.)
- If end to end Kerberos is required, you will need to use a Replication User.

How to Optimize SSL traffic

Overview

The SSL protocol is used to encrypt traffic at the application layer. Encrypted traffic normally cannot be compressed or de-duplicated by WAN optimization devices. But RiOS provides a mechanism for optimizing encrypted SSL traffic. This mechanism requires the import of the SSL server's certificate and private key into the server-side SteelHead appliance.

It's important to note that when optimizing SSL, the certificate and private key never leave the datacenter. They are installed on the server side SteelHead appliance only, much like an SSL-offload to a load balancer. This allows organizations to maintain security by not allowing private encryption keys to ever leave the data center. In addition, the SteelHead appliances will use SSL to encrypt the traffic between them across the WAN, so traffic always remains encrypted end to end across the network.

Get Valid SSL License for both Client and Server side SteelHead appliances

1. Go to **Configure > Maintenance > Licenses**.

Figure 5-20 *Licenses Page*

2. Check if "Enhanced Cryptographic License Key" is valid. If not, go to `https://support.riverbed.com` and click the link "Get a license to use the SSL optimization feature" to get a valid license key for SSL. You will need to have the serial number from your SteelHead appliance ready. The serial number can be found by clicking the **Support** menu on the SteelHead GUI.

Configure Client Side SteelHead Appliance

Port Labels
1. On client side SteelHead appliance, go to **Networking > App Definitions > Port Labels**.
2. Remove Port 443.

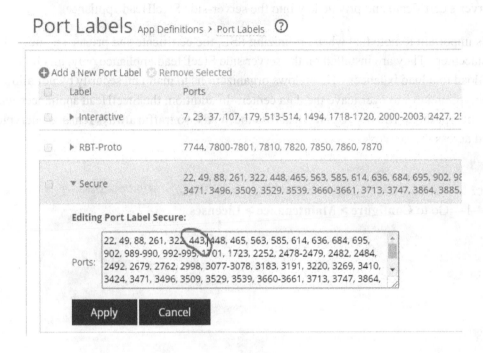

Figure 5-21 *Port Labels Page*

In-Path Rules
1. Go to **Optimization > Network Services > In-Path Rules**
2. Configure the In-Path Rule:

```
Preoptimization Policy = SSL
Latency Optimization Policy = HTTP
```

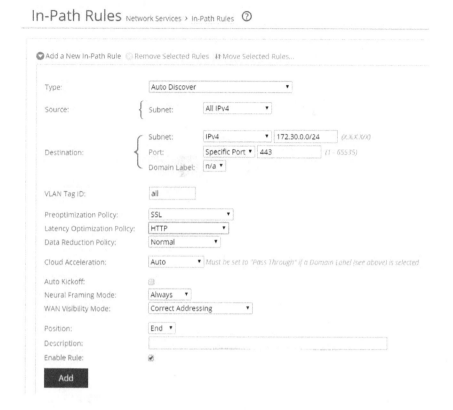

Figure 5-22 *In-Path Rules Page*

Configure SSL Main Settings

1. On both the client and server side SteelHead appliances, go to **Optimization > SSL > SSL Main Settings**.
2. Check on "Enable SSL Optimization" and Apply.
3. Restart optimization service.
4. On the server side SteelHead appliance add SSL Server Certificate for the SSL backend server(s).

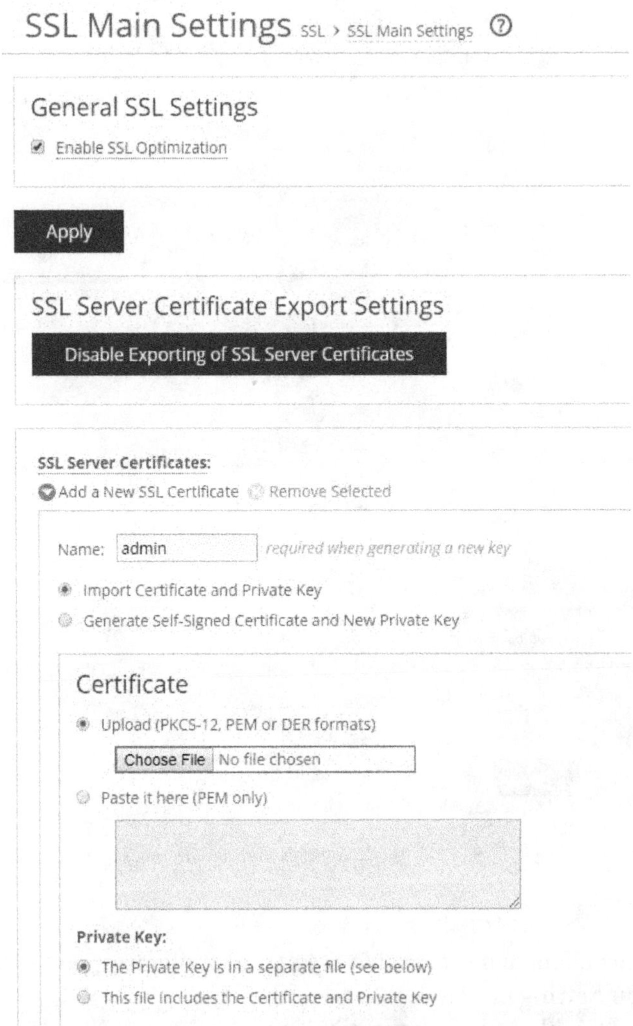

SSL Main Settings SSL › SSL Main Settings ⑦

General SSL Settings

☑ Enable SSL Optimization

[Apply]

SSL Server Certificate Export Settings

[Disable Exporting of SSL Server Certificates]

SSL Server Certificates:

⊕ Add a New SSL Certificate   ⊗ Remove Selected

Name: [admin]   *required when generating a new key*

● Import Certificate and Private Key
○ Generate Self-Signed Certificate and New Private Key

Certificate

● Upload (PKCS-12, PEM or DER formats)

[Choose File] No file chosen

○ Paste it here (PEM only)

Private Key:
● The Private Key is in a separate file (see below)
○ This file includes the Certificate and Private Key

Figure 5-23 *SSL Main Settings Page*

5. Add Certificate Authority's certificate.

Disable Verification of Issuer Certificates (if using self-signed certificate)

1. Login to SSH CLI and enter Configuration mode.
2. Enter:

```
#enable
#config term
#no protocol ssl backend server verify
```

Configure Mutual Peering Trust between SteelHead appliances

For each SteelHead appliance in the network perform the following:

1. Go to **Optimization > SSL > Secure Peering**.
2. Click PEM and copy certificate to clipboard. Paste into peer SteelHead appliance.

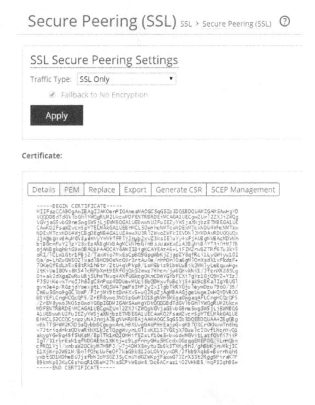

Figure 5-24 *SSL Secure Peering Page*

3. Restart Optimization service on both SteelHead appliances.
4. Verify in Current Connections Report that HTTP optimization to port 443 is working:

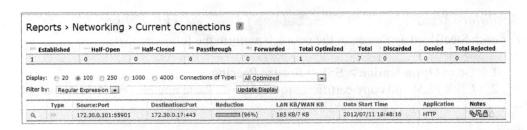

Figure 5-25 *Current Connections Report*

How to Deploy SteelHead SaaS

Overview

The major difference in configuring SteelHead SaaS optimization is that only the client side SteelHead is directly accessible. The server side SteelHead is a virtual instance that is managed by the cloud provider. Management of the server side instance is done indirectly from the Riverbed Cloud Portal. It is from the Cloud Portal where you can enable optimization for specific SaaS platforms and manage Proxy Certificates as explained in chapter 3.

Initial Requirements

Riverbed Cloud Portal Account

There are several important requirements that need to be fulfilled before beginning a SteelHead SaaS deployment. The first is to obtain an account in the Riverbed Cloud Portal. Every SteelHead SaaS customer should receive a Riverbed Cloud Portal account to deploy and manage their SteelHead SaaS solution. The portal can be reached at https://cloudportal.riverbed.com.

SSL License

A valid SSL license is required on the client side SteelHead in order to optimize HTTPS traffic to SaaS applications. Make sure the client side SteelHead(s) participating in SaaS optimization all have valid "Enhanced Cryptographic License Key" under the **Maintenance > Licenses** page.

Enable SSL

Make sure SSL is enabled on the client side SteelHead by going to the **Optimization > SSL Main Settings** page and checking on "Enable SSL Optimization."

Set Correct Date/Time

Make sure the correct Date/Time is configured on the client side SteelHead. You can configure the Date/Time in the **Administration > Date/Time** page.

Configure DNS Server

SteelHead SaaS needs a valid DNS Server in order to resolve the correct IP address not only for the correct SaaS destination but also for the correct Akamai Edge server. Go to **Networking > Host Settings** on the client side SteelHead to configure DNS servers.

Allow UDP 9545

SteelHead SaaS uses traffic encapsulated in UDP port 9545. Make sure firewalls allow both inbound and outbound traffic for UDP port 9545.

Appliance Registration

A client side SteelHead appliance must first be registered with the Cloud Portal before it can participate in SaaS optimization. Perform the following steps to register a SteelHead appliance:

Get Appliance Registration Key

1. Login to Riverbed Cloud Portal https://cloudportal.riverbed.com.
2. Click "View Company" for your company.
3. Click "Cloud Accelerator" tab.
4. Click "Appliance Registration Key" on the left side menu.
5. Copy the Registration Key. (Same key is used for all Steelheads in a company)

Figure 5-26 *Riverbed Cloud Portal*

Apply Registration Key to SteelHead Appliance(s)

1. Login to the client side Steelhead Appliance.
2. Go to **Optimization > SaaS > Cloud Accelerator** and enter the Registration Key.

Figure 5-27 *Appliance Registration Key Page*

3. Click "Register."

Grant Access to Steelhead from Cloud Portal

Once a SteelHead appliance is registered with the Cloud Portal, it needs to be granted service. Perform the following steps to grant service:

1. Login to Cloud Portal and click "Enterprise SteelHeads" from the left side menu.
2. Check SteelHeads Pending Service and click "Grant Service" to grant access to the Steelhead(s). (It can take a few minutes before the SteelHead satisfies all requirements for Cloud Acceleration.)

Figure 5-28 *SteelHeads Granted Service in Cloud Portal*

3. Once registered, Steelhead will download SaaS acceleration service data including peering certificates.
4. Click "SaaS Platforms" and click "Cloud Accelerator" to bring up "Manage SaaS Platforms." Check that Acceleration Service for your SaaS service is on. Click platform name for more details or to "Enable Acceleration."

Manage Saas Platforms

Click on a SaaS Platform to manage service settings and proxy certificates for that platform.

Service Group	Application Name (ID)	Acceleration Service
All-SaaS	Box (BOX)	☐ OFF
All-SaaS	Microsoft Dynamics CRM (DCRM)	☐ OFF
All-SaaS	Office 365 (O365)	☑ ON
All-SaaS	Office 365 Web Apps (O365OWA)	☑ ON
All-SaaS	Office 365 User Identity (SAASUID)	☑ ON
All-SaaS	Salesforce.com (SFDC)	☑ ON
All-SaaS	SuccessFactors (SFSF)	☐ OFF
All-SaaS	ServiceNow (SVCNOW)	☐ OFF
All-SaaS	Veeva (VEEVA)	☑ ON

Figure 5-29 *Manage SaaS Platforms from Cloud Portal*

5. From the Steelhead appliance, go to **SaaS > Cloud Accelerator > Application Control** and enable your SaaS Applications:

SaaS Application Control	Application ID	Service Group	Local Optimization
Office 365 User Identity	SAASUID	All-SaaS	Enabled ▾
Salesforce.com	SFDC	All-SaaS	Enabled ▾
Office 365	O365	All-SaaS	Enabled ▾
Veeva	VEEVA	All-SaaS	Disabled ▾
Office 365 Web Apps	O365OWA	All-SaaS	Enabled ▾

Figure 5-30 *Enable SaaS Applications from Cloud Portal*

Configure Cloud Acceleration Redirection on Steelhead

The client side SteelHead appliance now needs to be enabled to redirect SaaS application traffic to the Akamai cloud.

1. Log back into Steelhead and go to **Optimization > Cloud Accelerator**.

2. Check "Enable Cloud Acceleration Redirection" to send optimization probe directly to Akamai. (Direct Mode) By checking this on, the SteelHead will encapsulate SaaS application traffic in UDP port 9545 and send to Akamai cloud.

3. Check **OFF** on Branch SteelHead if using **backhaul mode**. (If using backhaul mode, the DC Steelhead must also be registered with the Cloud Portal and have this checked **ON**.)

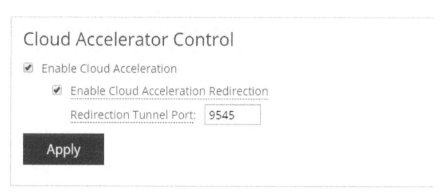

Figure 5-31 *Enable Cloud Acceleration Redirection*

Configure In-Path rules on SteelHead

Since SaaS applications are accessed using HTTPS, don't forget to configure client side SteelHead in-path rule to optimize HTTPS traffic:

1. From client side SteelHead go to **Optimization > In-Path rules**.
2. Set Preoptimization Policy to "SSL."
3. Set Latency Optimization Policy to "Normal." (Normal setting allows SteelHead to auto detect correct optimization module.)
4. Set Cloud Acceleration to "Auto."

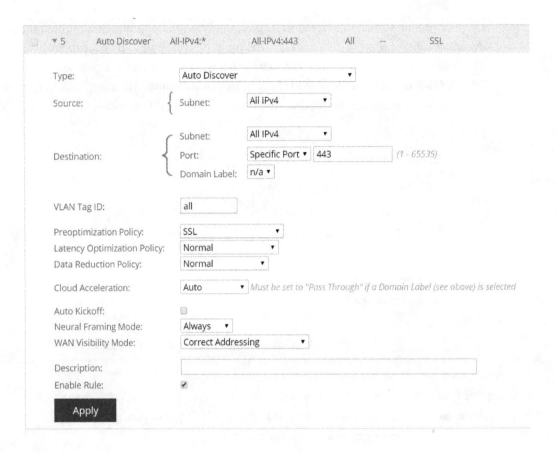

Figure 5-32 *In-Path Rule for SaaS*

Configure MAPI (for O365 traffic only)

If accessing email via Office 365, you will need to configure MAPI optimization on the client side SteelHead.

1. On client side Steelhead go to **Configure >Optimization Protocols > MAPI**.
2. Check on "Enable Outlook Anywhere Optimization", "Auto-Detect Outlook Anywhere Connections" and "Enable Encrypted Optimization."

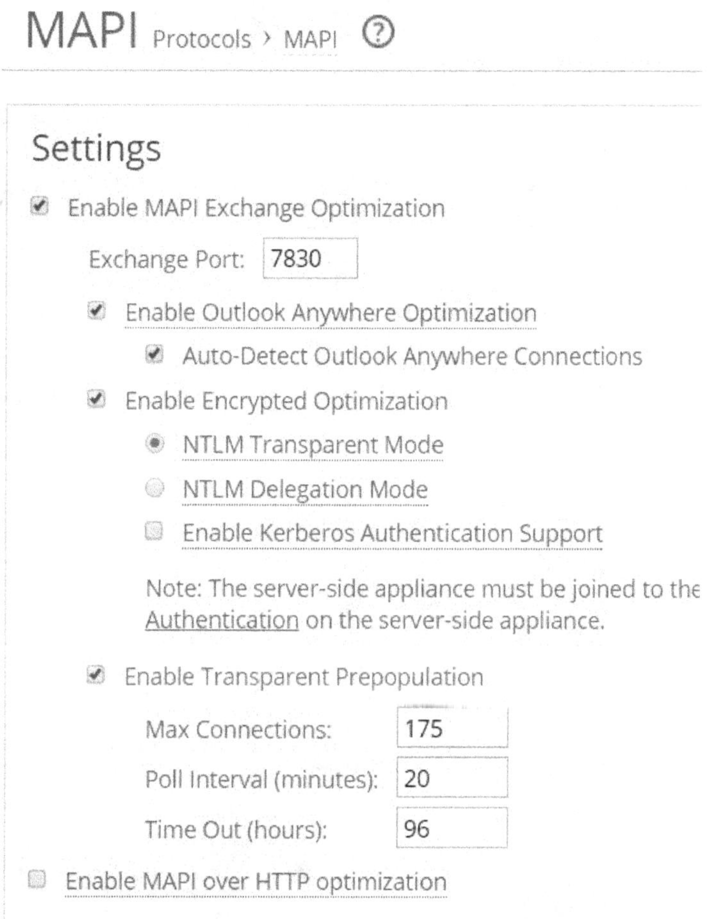

MAPI Protocols › MAPI ⑦

Settings

☑ Enable MAPI Exchange Optimization

Exchange Port: 7830

☑ Enable Outlook Anywhere Optimization

☑ Auto-Detect Outlook Anywhere Connections

☑ Enable Encrypted Optimization

◉ NTLM Transparent Mode

○ NTLM Delegation Mode

☐ Enable Kerberos Authentication Support

Note: The server-side appliance must be joined to the Authentication on the server-side appliance.

☑ Enable Transparent Prepopulation

Max Connections: 175

Poll Interval (minutes): 20

Time Out (hours): 96

☐ Enable MAPI over HTTP optimization

Figure 5-33 *Enable Encrypted Optimization for MAPI*

Trust Enterprise SteelHead Peering Certificates

The client side SteelHead and Akamai cloud need to exchange SSL certificates in order to establish a trusted peering relationship. Perform the following steps to establish a trusted peering relationship between a client side SteelHead and Akamai Cloud SteelHeads:

1. Login to Cloud Portal and click "Secure Peering."
2. Click "Peering Certificates" tab.
3. Check on "Trust Enterprise Steelhead Peering Certificates." Steelhead will upload peering certificate to Cloud Portal and download certificate from Cloud Portal.

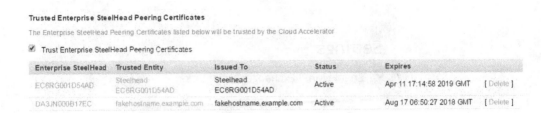

Figure 5-34 *Trust Enterprise Peering Certificates*

4. Click **Cloud-Hosted Peering CA** tab to confirm to confirm Steelhead has downloaded peer CA.

Figure 5-35 *Cloud-Hosted Peering CA*

5. Confirm Service Ready is "Yes" on Steelhead. (May take a few minutes)
6. Enable Local Optimization for SaaS Application(s)

Figure 5-36 *Enable Local Optimization for SaaS Application(s)*

Configure Proxy Certificates

As explained earlier in chapter 3, SteelHead SaaS requires the use of Proxy Certificates in order to decrypt, optimize and re-encrypt SaaS traffic running over HTTPS. Proxy Certificates are generated by Akamai and they emulate the real certificate of the SaaS provider.

Generate CA Certificate

A Proxy Certificates must be signed either by a customer's own internal certificate authority (CA) or by Akamai's CA. Use the Cloud Portal to generate the CA certificate.

1. Login to Riverbed Cloud Portal.
2. Click "SaaS Platforms."
3. Under **Proxy Certificate Authority** select a **Certificate Authority Mode**.

98

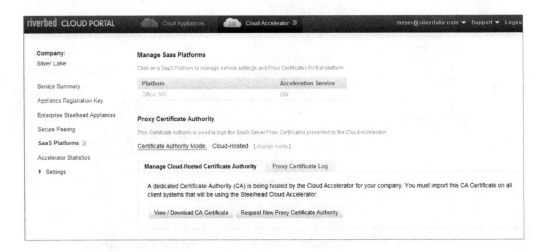

Figure 5-37 *Certificate Authority Mode*

4. If using Cloud-Hosted CA, click **"change mode"** and select "Cloud-Hosted CA" mode to download CA Certificate. Click on "Request New Proxy for Certificate Authority" and enter certificate details. Click "Save on Details" after entering certificate info.
5. If using Customer CA, click **"change mode"** and select "Customer CA" mode and click Update.

Figure 5-38 *Select "Customer CA"*

Generate Proxy Certificate(s)
Now it's time to generate a Proxy Certificate for each SaaS destination.

1. Go to **Settings > Certificate Settings** and fill out Certificate info.

Figure 5-39 *Proxy Certificate Details*

2. Click on SaaS Platform to bring up **Manage SaaS Platforms**.

Manage Saas Platforms

Click on a SaaS Platform to manage service settings and proxy certificates for that platform.

Service Group	Application Name (ID)	Acceleration Service
All-SaaS	Box (BOX)	OFF
All-SaaS	Microsoft Dynamics CRM (DCRM)	OFF
All-SaaS	Office 365 (O365)	ON
All-SaaS	Office 365 Web Apps (O365OWA)	ON
All-SaaS	Office 365 User Identity (SAASUID)	ON
All-SaaS	Salesforce.com (SFDC)	ON
All-SaaS	SuccessFactors (SFSF)	OFF
All-SaaS	ServiceNow (SVCNOW)	OFF
All-SaaS	Veeva (VEEVA)	OFF

Figure 5-40 *Manage SaaS Platforms from Cloud Portal*

3. Click on an Application Name to bring up **SaaS Platform Proxy Certificates**.

4. If using **Cloud Hosted CA**, click "Request New Proxy Certificate" to generate a Proxy Certificate for specific hostnames. You can generate multiple certificates at the same time. A new proxy certificate can take up to 30 minutes to create.

Hostname	Proxy Certificate Status	Expires	
*.cs8.force.com	---		[Request New Proxy Certificate]
*.na5.force.com	---		[Request New Proxy Certificate]
ap.salesforce.com	---		[Request New Proxy Certificate]
*.my.salesforce.com	---		[Request New Proxy Certificate]
na1.salesforce.com	---		[Request New Proxy Certificate]
*.cs1.my.salesforce.com	---		[Request New Proxy Certificate]
na12.salesforce.com	---		[Request New Proxy Certificate]
cs10.salesforce.com	---		[Request New Proxy Certificate]
emea.salesforce.com	---		[Request New Proxy Certificate]
*.na6.force.com	---		[Request New Proxy Certificate]

Figure 5-41 *Request New Proxy Certificate*

5. If using **Customer CA,** click "Generate New CSR." Download the CSR and then upload the signed Certificate. (This can take 15 minutes or more.)

SaaS Platform Proxy Certificates

This section is used to manage trust between your client machines and the SteelHead Cloud Accelerator. Y
systems. You then upload the resulting signed Proxy Certificate to the SteelHead Cloud Accelerator.

| Proxy Certificates | Certificate Signing Request Log |

Step 1: Generate Certificate Signing Request for specific SaaS Hostnames

Filter: [   ] Clear

<< first < prev   **1**   next > last >>

Hostname	CSR Status
*.vod309.com	Generate CSR Request sent at 2018-03-26 03:49:42 UTC

Step 2: Download Certificate Signing Request

Step 3: Upload Signed Certificate

Filter: [   ] Clear

<< first < prev   next > last >>

Hostname	Proxy Certificate Status
No records found.	

Figure 5-42 *Generate New CSR*

Install CA Certificate on Client(s)

Once the certificates are generated you will need to install the CA certificate on each client machine that needs to participate in SaaS optimization. Check the documentation for your operating system (i.e. Windows or MacOS) for detailed instructions on installing a CA certificate on your system.

Verify Optimization

The best way to verify that SaaS optimization is working properly is to run the Current Connections report on the client side SteelHead. But first it is recommended that you check on "Enable Application Visibility" in the Flow Statistics page.

Enable Application Visibility

1. From Client SteelHead go to **Networking > Flow Statistics**.
2. Check ON "Enable Application Visibility."

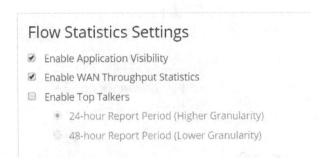

Figure 5-43 *Enable Application Visibility*

Run Current Connections Report

In this example we are verifying that optimization to SharePoint Online is working properly:

1. Login to client side SteelHead and go to Current Connections report.
2. You should see optimized connection with cloud symbol:

Figure 5-44 *Optimized connection with cloud symbol*

SteelHead Advanced Networking Features

RiOS comes with several important networking features that make it easier to deploy SteelHead appliances into certain types of network environments.

Simplified Routing

What it does

Simplified Routing is a networking feature used to prevent packet ricochet. Packet ricochet occurs when a packet travels through the same SteelHead appliance more than once. This can occur if a host is located on a different subnet from the SteelHead appliance and a gateway exists between the SteelHead appliance and the host. For instance, if there is a gateway on the SteelHead appliance's LAN side, a packet can be forwarded to this gateway and then routed back to a destination on the SteelHead appliance's WAN side causing the packet to travel through the SteelHead appliance a second time.

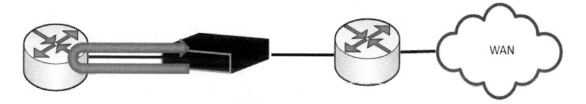

Figure 5-45 *Packet Ricochet*

Packet ricochet is undesirable because it can degrade network performance and potentially cause packets to be dropped by certain firewalls. When Simplified Routing is enabled, the SteelHead appliance is able to select the correct destination Ethernet address for optimized traffic so that packets do not ricochet back through the same SteelHead appliance.

How it Works

Simplified Routing uses a mapping of IP addresses to MAC addresses from which the correct next hop destination can be selected. This mapping of IP address to MAC address is collected every time a packet passes through the SteelHead appliance. When a packet enters the SteelHead appliance's LAN or WAN interface, the SteelHead appliance will examine the source and destination addresses on the packet and "learn" which IP address is associated with which MAC address. The SteelHead appliance can then use this mapping to select the correct destination MAC address for a given destination IP address. With Simplified Routing, there is no need to add static routes to the SteelHead appliance in order to ensure that packets are routed through the correct network interface.

Configuration

Simplified Routing is enabled by default in RiOS. To configure Simplified Routing go to **Configure > Networking > Simplified Routing** on the Management Console. There are four options for Simplified Routing under the "Collect Mappings From" drop down list:

None

Do not collect mappings for Simplified Routing. This effectively disables Simplified Routing.

Destination Only

Only collect mappings for destination IP address to MAC address.

Destination and Source

Collect mapping for both source and destination addresses.

All

This option is same as "Destination and Source" except that it also collects mappings from non-optimized or pass-through traffic too.

Best Practices

Simplified Routing is enabled by default. The default setting is to collect mappings from "Destination Only." This default setting is recommended for most in-path deployments where the SteelHead appliance is deployed between a LAN switch and a WAN router. "Destination Only" is also recommended in asymmetric routing environments.

Use "Source and Destination" or "All" if the client and server are on different subnets and a gateway exists on the LAN side of the SteelHead appliance. This will ensure that packets destined for a peer SteelHead appliance will be mapped to the WAN side of the SteelHead appliance.

Source mappings should not be used in connection forwarding environments where optimized connections are forwarded from one SteelHead appliance to another within the same LAN. Mappings should be collected from destination only instead in connection forwarding environments.

Simplified Routing should not be used with Layer-2 broadcast WANs. You must use static routes to override the learned routes in Simplified Routing. To override simplified routing use the following CLI command:

```
>in-path simplified mac-def-gw-only
```

Enhanced Auto Discovery

What it does

Enhanced Auto Discovery is used to ensure that a SteelHead appliance in the middle of two outer SteelHead appliances does not automatically respond to an auto discovery probe and optimize a connection. Enhanced Auto discovery makes sure that the last SteelHead appliance in a connection peers with the first SteelHead appliance to optimize a connection.

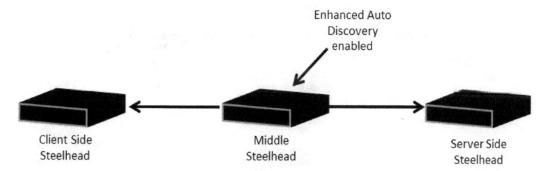

Figure 5-46 *Enhanced Auto Discovery*

How it Works

If Enhanced Auto Discovery is enabled, a SteelHead appliance receiving an auto discovery probe (0x4c) inside a TCP SYN packet will attach another 0x4c probe to the packet and pass it on to the destination. If the SteelHead appliance then receives a probe response from the SteelHead appliance it then knows it is not the last SteelHead appliance in the network path of the connection. It will pass on the packets for the connection without optimization.

Configuration

To enable Enhanced Auto Discovery go **to Configure > Optimization > Peering Rules** in the Management Console.

Best Practices

Enhanced Auto Discover is enabled by default. The recommended best practice is to leave it enabled on all SteelHeads. It should only be disabled if optimization between an outer SteelHead appliance and a middle SteelHead appliance is desired. (This is not common.)

WAN Visibility

What it does

The WAN visibility feature in RiOS allows you to control what IP addresses and ports are visible in the inner connection between the SteelHead appliances.

The SteelHead appliances by default use correct addressing. In correct addressing the original client and server IP addresses are translated into the SteelHead appliance IP addresses and the destination port number is translated to 7800.

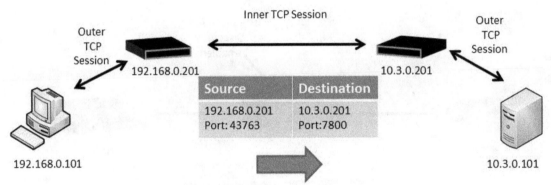

Figure 5-47 *Correct Addressing*

Correct addressing works fine in most network environments; using the IP addresses of the devices which are communicating makes it easier to avoid asymmetric routing causing connections to go the wrong place. But sometimes a QoS device or firewall on the WAN side of the SteelHead appliance will expect to see the original and not the NATted IP addresses. In such cases, the WAN visibility feature can be used to preserve the original IP and port numbers across the WAN. RiOS provides four different WAN visibility modes:

Correct Addressing

SteelHead appliances use SteelHead appliance IP and server port (7800) for inner connections.

Port Transparency
SteelHead appliances preserve original destination ports but still use SteelHead appliance IPs. (It does not preserve the original client port.)

Full Transparency
SteelHead appliances preserve both source and destination IPs and port numbers.

Full Transparency with Forward Reset
SteelHead appliances preserve both source and destination IPs and port numbers. In addition, TCP reset packets are sent across the WAN during auto discovery. This is sometimes needed to integrate with stateful firewalls deployed in between the SteelHead appliances.

How it works
When using port or full transparency, the client side SteelHead appliance will insert a probe (0x78) into the TCP options field of the packet headers. It will also insert its own in-path IP address. When a server-side SteelHead appliance sees the probe it will know the packet belongs to an optimized connection as well as the client side SteelHead appliance's IP. This allows the SteelHead appliances to discover and peer with each other without using their actual IP addresses.

Transparency mode will only work with physically in-path SteelHead appliances. It will not work with SteelHead appliances deployed out of path.

Configuration
To configure WAN visibility go to **Optimization > Network Services > In-Path Rules** on the client side SteelHead appliance. Click the "Add a New In-Path Rule" tab and select "Auto Discovery" type rule. Down below will be a drop down list where you can select the WAN visibility Mode for a connection.

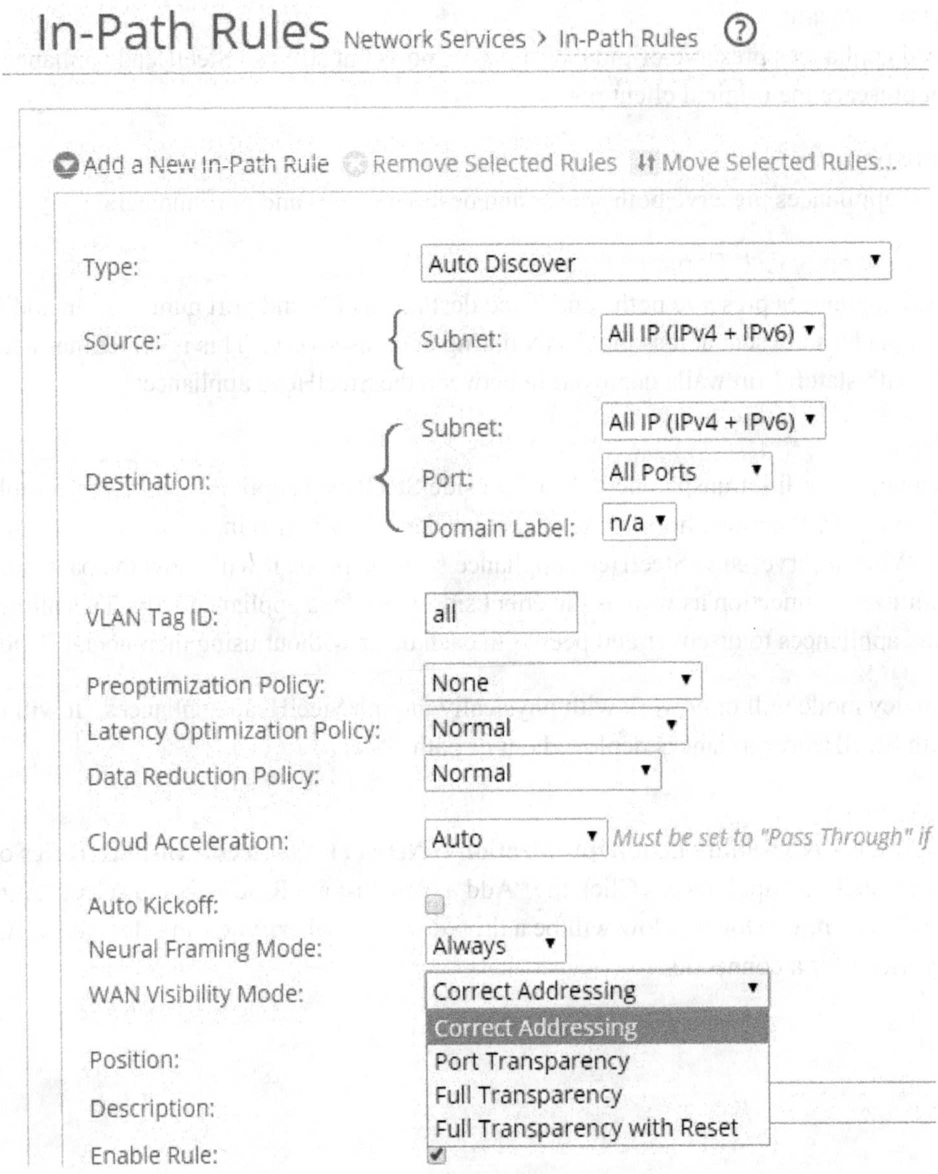

In-Path Rules Network Services › In-Path Rules ⑦

⊙ Add a New In-Path Rule ⊙ Remove Selected Rules ↕ Move Selected Rules...

Type:	Auto Discover	▼
Source:	Subnet:	All IP (IPv4 + IPv6) ▼
Destination:	Subnet:	All IP (IPv4 + IPv6) ▼
	Port:	All Ports ▼
	Domain Label:	n/a ▼
VLAN Tag ID:	all	
Preoptimization Policy:	None ▼	
Latency Optimization Policy:	Normal ▼	
Data Reduction Policy:	Normal ▼	
Cloud Acceleration:	Auto ▼	*Must be set to "Pass Through" if*
Auto Kickoff:	☐	
Neural Framing Mode:	Always ▼	
WAN Visibility Mode:	Correct Addressing ▼	
	Correct Addressing	
Position:	Port Transparency	
Description:	Full Transparency	
Enable Rule:	Full Transparency with Reset	
	☑	

Figure 5-48 *WAN Visibility Mode*

Best Practices

The SteelHead appliances by default use correct addressing. Port and full transparency mode should only be used if QoS devices or firewalls on the WAN side of the SteelHead appliance require or expect to see the original IPs or port numbers. A potential problem of using transparency modes is that if packets for an optimized connection get misrouted, they may bypass a server-side SteelHead appliance altogether and reach the destination server. Since the packet payload will not be in native format, the packets will be rejected causing the connection to be reset.

110

Chapter 6: Troubleshooting SteelHead appliances

This chapter gives tips on troubleshooting common problems when installing and configuring SteelHead appliances. We begin with diagnostic tools on the SteelHead appliance that can provide useful information for troubleshooting problems. We then give tips for troubleshooting common optimization and networking issues.

Troubleshooting Tools

System Logs

SteelHead appliance Systems Logs are usually the first place to look for error messages that can help you identify the cause of common SteelHead appliance issues. You can access the System Logs by going to **Reports > Diagnostics > System Logs**.

Figure 6-1 *System Logs*

You can also download the System Logs as a text file by going to **Reports > Diagnostics > System Logs Download**.

There are seven different levels of severity for log messages. "Info" is the lowest severity level and "Emergency" is the highest. You can configure the level of severity logged in the System Logs by going to **Administration > System Settings > Logging**.

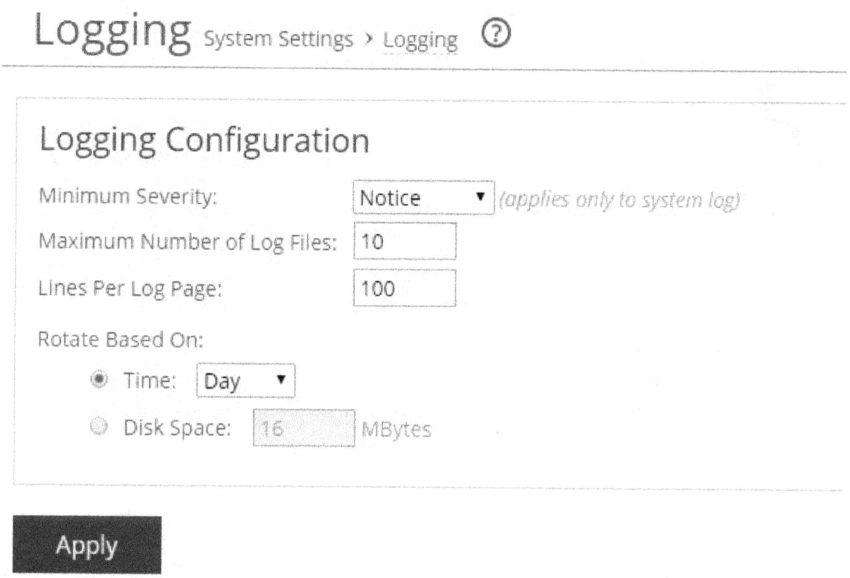

Logging System Settings > Logging ⑦

Logging Configuration

Minimum Severity: Notice ▾ *(applies only to system log)*

Maximum Number of Log Files: 10

Lines Per Log Page: 100

Rotate Based On:

◉ Time: Day ▾

○ Disk Space: 16 MBytes

Apply

Figure 6-2 *Logging Configuration*

The SteelHead appliance will log any messages at the specified Minimum Severity level or higher. The default Minimum Severity level is set to "Notice." It is recommended that when troubleshooting most issues that the Minimum Severity level be temporarily set to "Info" to capture the most amount of information. The Minimum Severity level should then be set back to "Notice" after troubleshooting to conserve log space.

Network Health Check

The Network Health Check tool is very useful for troubleshooting common networking issues. You can access Health Check by going to **Reports > Diagnostics > Network Health Check**.

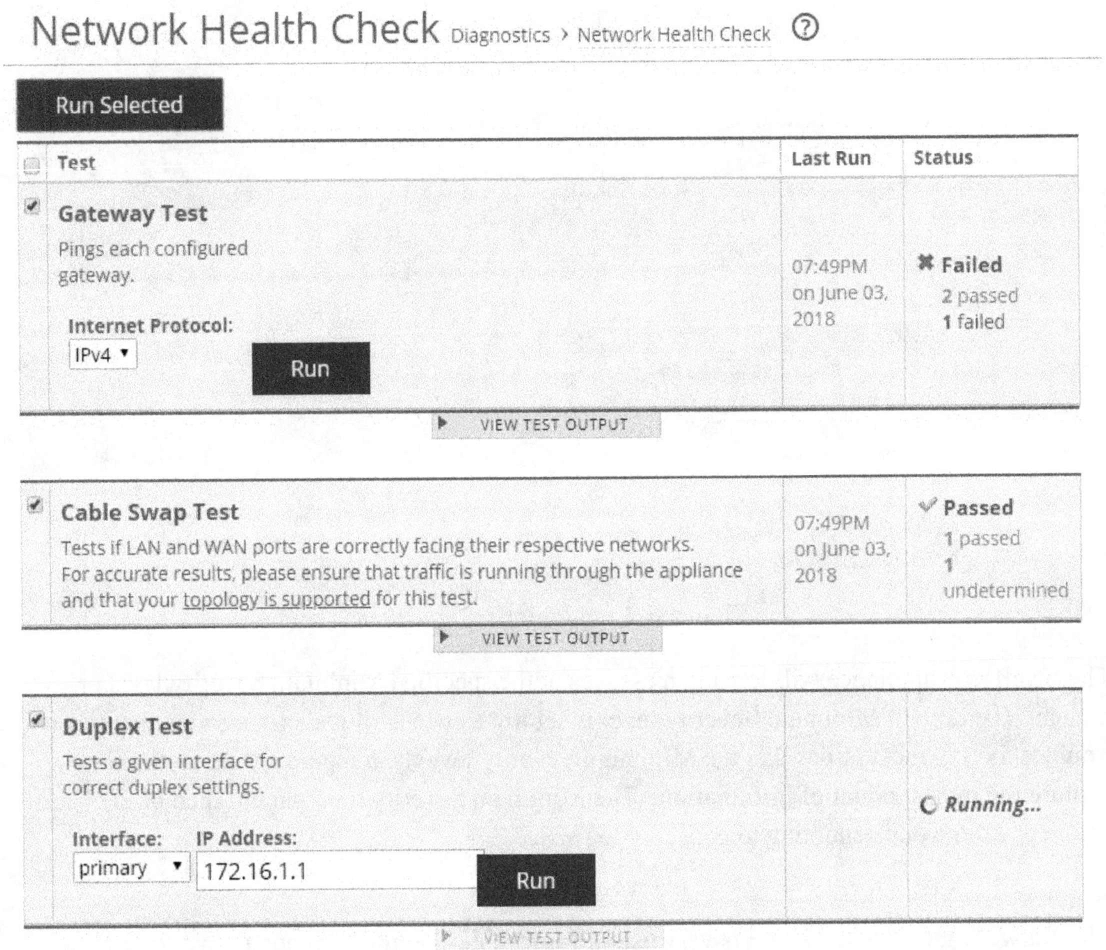

Network Health Check Diagnostics › Network Health Check ⑦

	Test		Last Run	Status
☑	**Gateway Test** Pings each configured gateway. **Internet Protocol:** IPv4 ▾ [Run]		07:49PM on June 03, 2018	✖ **Failed** 2 passed 1 failed
☑	**Cable Swap Test** Tests if LAN and WAN ports are correctly facing their respective networks. For accurate results, please ensure that traffic is running through the appliance and that your <u>topology is supported</u> for this test.		07:49PM on June 03, 2018	✔ **Passed** 1 passed 1 undetermined
☑	**Duplex Test** Tests a given interface for correct duplex settings. **Interface:** primary ▾ **IP Address:** 172.16.1.1 [Run]			↻ *Running...*

[Run Selected]

▸ VIEW TEST OUTPUT

▸ VIEW TEST OUTPUT

▸ VIEW TEST OUTPUT

Figure 6-3 *Network Health Check*

Gateway Test
Use the Gateway Test to test the SteelHead appliance's connectivity to the default gateway.

Cable Swap Test
Use the Cable Swap Test if you suspect the cables going to the LAN and the WAN interfaces are reversed. There must be traffic going through the SteelHead appliance for this test to work and it is not always 100% accurate. If it detects a large number of connections coming from the WAN side, the test guesses that the cables are reversed.

Duplex Test

Use the duplex test if you suspect that there is a mismatch between the speed and duplex settings on the SteelHead appliance NICs and an interface on the other side. You need to enter an IP address on the other side of the SteelHead appliance NIC. This test works by sending out pings and reports failure if packets are lost.

Peer Reachability Test

Use this test to check if a peer SteelHead appliance is reachable. You enter the IP address of the peer SteelHead appliance for this test.

IP-Port Reachability Test

Use this to test connectivity to a specific IP address and port.

System Dump

Sometimes a System Dump from the SteelHead appliance is requested by Riverbed Support in order to troubleshoot an advanced issue. The System Dump includes detailed logging and system info from the SteelHead appliance that is readable only by Riverbed Support personnel. To generate a System Dump go to **Reports > Diagnostics > System Dumps**.

TCP Dump

The SteelHead appliance can generate TCP Dump files to allow analysis of packets that flow through the SteelHead appliance network interfaces. These packet capture files can be downloaded and then analyzed by Wireshark. Packets can also be accessed directly on the SteelHead appliance through Cascade Pilot. To generate TCP dumps go to **Reports > Diagnostics > TCP Dumps.**

Optimization Issues

TCP Traffic not being optimized

You can verify whether individual connections going through the SteelHead appliance are optimized or not by going to **Reports > Networking > Current Connections**. If a connection you expect to be optimized is showing up as pass through or un-optimized try the following:

- Is a Cisco PIX or ASA firewall being used? If so, the RiOS auto discovery probe is probably being stripped. Use a fixed-target rule or refer to Riverbed Support's Knowledgebase for instructions on how to configure the firewall.
- Make sure firewalls are allowing traffic to port 7800 or 7810.
- Can the SteelHead appliance in-path IP addresses ping each other? If not, check routing between the appliances.
- Is the SteelHead appliance on a VLAN trunk? If so, make sure correct VLAN Tag ID is specified in the In-Path Rule by going to **Optimization > Network Services > In-Path Rules**.
- Check for asymmetrical routing. Make sure traffic isn't bypassing the SteelHead appliance on client or server side.
- Check if the destination port is in a Port Label that is being passed through in one of the In Path Rules.
- RiOS by default will not optimize existing connections. If the connection already existed when Service started, try closing and re-establishing the connection. You can also reset the connection from the Current Connections report by clicking the magnifying glass at the left of each connection and clicking the "Reset Connection" button.
- Check if the connections are local or to other sites that do not have a SteelHead appliance deployed.

Getting 0% data reduction for MAPI traffic

Sometimes the Current Connections report will show 0% data reduction for MAPI traffic.

- 0% data reduction almost always indicates that the traffic is encrypted. See section on "How to Optimized Secure Windows Traffic" in chapter 5.

Getting Protocol Errors for CIFS/SMB traffic

Sometimes the Current Connections report will show a red triangle indicating a protocol error for a CIFS/SMB connection.

- Click the magnifying glass for the connection in the Current Connections report to get reason for the protocol error.

- Protocol errors from CIFS traffic usually occur if SMB signing is in use. See section on "How to Optimized Signed SMB and Encrypted MAPI traffic."
- If error is SMBv2 related make sure SMBv2 optimization is enabled in **Optimization > Protocols > SMB2/3.**

SSL Optimization not working

- Check System Logs. Make sure client is using SSLv3 or TLSv1.
- Make sure SSL license on the SteelHead appliances are valid by going to **Configure > Maintenance > Licenses**.
- Make sure to import the Certificate Authority certificate into the server side SteelHead appliance. If using self-signed certificates disable verification of the SSL certificate by entering this CLI command on the server side SteelHead appliance:

```
(config)# no protocol ssl backend server verify
```

- Go to **Configure > Optimization > SSL Main Settings**. Check if the SSL server appears in the bypassed server list. If so, check that the Server Common Name matches the CN in the SSL certificate.
- Check In-Path rules. Make sure an Auto Intercept or fixed-target rule is enabled for the SSL traffic.
- Check network connection between SteelHead appliances. Make sure LAN/WAN cables are not reversed. If using In-Path deployment, make sure the In-Path IP addresses can connect to each other.

Cold Transfer is slower than un-optimized pass-through traffic

- This can sometimes occur if the optimized WAN capacity of the SteelHead appliance is less than the available bandwidth. The SteelHead appliance may need to be re-sized to a larger appliance.

SaaS Optimization not working

- Make sure firewalls allow UDP:**9545** traffic to and from the Steelhead In-Path IP. You can run #udpcheck from SteelHead CLI.
- Sometimes it takes a few minutes for the ACSH to spin up.
- Use ping to confirm connectivity from InPath IP to destination.
- Make sure SteelHead Mobile client optimization is disabled.
- Make sure NTP on the Steelhead is enabled with correct time.
- Make sure Proxy Certificate(s) are requested for SaaS hostname(s).
- Make sure Steelhead is configured with valid DNS entries.

- If using dogfood portal enter following CLI command on SteelHead:
  ```
  (config) #service cloud-accel portal host "aws-cloud-df.riverbed.com" port 443
  protocol https
  ```
- Check that SSL peering certificates are still valid. If you just generated a new one, it can take a few minutes for it to upload to the cloud portal.
- From the Cloud Portal, go to **Enterprise SteelHeads** and click the SteelHead serial number to check that requirements for Cloud Acceleration have been met:

Figure 6-4 *Acceleration Status*

Networking Issues

Duplex Errors

- Try setting the WAN interface to 100mb/full which is the speed and duplex of most routers. If the speed and duplex of the router is set to 100 Full, then set the SteelHead to 100 Full.
- Make sure a crossover cable is used between WAN interface and router.
- Is there a Layer 3 device connected on LAN side? Make sure it is connected with a crossover cable.
- Check if router model supports full/duplex. It may only support half duplex.

Cannot Join Windows Domain

- Make sure server-side SteelHead appliance primary IP is in DNS.

- Make sure SteelHead appliance clock and Domain Server clock are within 30 seconds of each other.
- Make sure DNS Server is entered in the SteelHead appliance.
- Make sure domain login is entered correctly.
- Make sure Primary interface has a connection to the AD server.
- Restart the service after enabling SMB signing.
- Enter Short Domain Name if NetBIOS name differs from first portion of AD name.
- Make sure SteelHead appliance hostname is 15 characters or less in length.

Asymmetric Routing Detected

SteelHead appliances cannot optimize connections that are asymmetrically routed. Asymmetric routing occurs when the packets in a TCP connection do not pass through both the client and server side SteelHead appliances in both directions. In other words, at least one of the SteelHead appliances is bypassed. This can occur if there are multiple routes between the client and server and the SteelHead appliance is deployed inline in only one of these routes. Asymmetric routing can easily occur in data centers that have redundant routers or switches. If the SteelHead appliance is not inline between all routers and switches then asymmetric routing may occur.

Asymmetric routing is detected by the client side SteelHead appliance. The following are three types of asymmetrical routing that can be detected by the client side SteelHead appliance:

- Client Side Asymmetry – the client side SteelHead appliance is bypassed on the return trip. Indicated when no SYN/ACK is received.
- Server Side Asymmetry – the server side SteelHead appliance is bypassed. Indicated when a bad SYN/ACK is received from the server.
- Complete Asymmetry – both client and server side SteelHead appliance is bypassed on return trip. Indicated by a bad RST from the client.

Go to **Configure > Networking > Asymmetric Routing** to see list of detected asymmetric routes. Check the source and destination IPs. Do these connections need to be optimized? Or are they connections to sites that do not have a SteelHead appliance? Asymmetric routes to sites that do not have a SteelHead appliance are normal. If asymmetric routes are detected for connections that are expected to be optimized then you may need to re-examine your network topology and use a SteelHead appliance with multiple LAN/WAN interfaces.

Suggestions for Further Reading

In this book we have covered the basics of WAN Optimization with Riverbed. Hopefully, you now have an understanding of the benefits of WAN Optimization and how you can use Riverbed SteelHead appliances to accelerate important applications across the WAN.

Although we have covered the basics, no two networking environments are exactly alike. And as you implement WAN optimization for your organization, you may encounter a design or integration issue that was not covered in this book. With that we conclude with suggestions for further reading:

Riverbed Technology, *SteelHead Appliance Deployment Guide*.

This is the best and most complete resource for deploying the SteelHead appliance. This guide covers almost all the networking and deployment scenarios you are likely to encounter. It is updated regularly by Riverbed and can be downloaded from the Riverbed Support site.

Riverbed Technology, *SteelHead Appliance Installation and Configuration Guide*.

This provides detailed step by step instructions for installing a SteelHead appliance for the first time. It is also updated regularly by Riverbed and can be downloaded from the Riverbed Support site.

Riverbed Technology, *SteelHead Management Console User's Guide*.

This describes how to manage and configure the SteelHead appliance using its GUI. It also has an important chapter on how to read and interpret SteelHead appliance reports. This guide is also updated regularly by Riverbed and can be downloaded from the Riverbed Support site.

Smoot, Stephen R. and Nam K Tan. *Private Cloud Computing*. Waldham: Elsevier, 2011.

WAN optimization is a critical component of private cloud computing. Written by senior networking experts from Riverbed, this book explains how WAN optimization is integrated with other key virtualization and storage technologies to consolidate infrastructure into a private cloud.